Aga
cooking

AGA

Aga
cooking

the contemporary bible for all Aga owners

Amy Willcock

EBURY PRESS
LONDON

Dedication
To my parents, Iris and Bart.

First published in Great Britain in 2002

1 3 5 7 9 10 8 6 4 2

First published by Ebury Press
Random House, 20 Vauxhall Bridge Road,
London SW1V 2SA

Random House Australia (Pty) Limited
20 Alfred Street, Milsons Point, Sydney,
New South Wales 2061, Australia

Random House New Zealand Limited
18 Poland Road, Glenfield, Auckland 10, New Zealand

Random House South Africa (Pty) Limited
Endulini, 5A Jubilee Road, Parktown 2193, South Africa

The Random House Group Limited Reg. No. 954009

www.randomhouse.co.uk

A CIP catalogue record for this book is available from the
British Library.

Editor: Gillian Haslam
Designer: Christine Wood
Photographer: William Lingwood
Props stylist: Helen Trent
Food styling: Fork Ltd

Photographs p8 and p11 courtesy of Aga-Rayburn.
Photograph p14 © Mitch Jenkins.
Diagrams p9 and 10 courtesy of Aga-Rayburn.

ISBN 0 09 188621 X

Printed and bound in Singapore by Tien Wah Press

contents

Introduction

Owning an Aga really does become a way of life – it is a trusted friend in the kitchen. I adore cooking with my Aga and wouldn't dream of having anything else.

Kitchens are dynamic centres of living in modern homes. Today, we live in our kitchens. A comfortable sofa is now as important as a fridge. Friends, children and pets all gravitate to the kitchen whether it is for eating, doing homework or grabbing an espresso. The kitchen has truly become the heart of the home, not just a place to prepare food, and one of the most coveted objects in a kitchen is an Aga.

I spend a lot of time extolling the virtues of Aga cooking and telling non-believers that Agas are not just for casseroles and shepherd's pies, but are also terrific for risotto and low-fat cooking. It's bliss to take a roll of ready-made cookie dough from the freezer and have freshly baked hazelnut chocolate chip cookies in exactly 12 minutes. Because an Aga is always ready to use, there is no need to wait around for ovens to heat up.

The demands of modern living mean we need quick and easy food for every day of the week, so in

fast food... easy food... a

fast, simple, elaborate, any food is aga food

this book there are recipes that will enable you to put delicious food on the table with the minimum of effort and time. In other chapters, you will also find recipes ranging from roasting a traditional Christmas turkey to making Neapolitan pizza for a quick supper for friends, plus ideas for making tempting food for children. As well as old favourites, such as shepherd's pie and fruit crumble, you'll find plenty of up-to-date modern recipes, such as stir-fried chicken and noodles, hot tuna salad, prawn and pumpkin curry, crispy duck pancakes and focaccia bread.

Aga Cooking is a fresh, modern, relaxed approach to cooking and using an Aga in today's world. Cooking has changed dramatically in the last ten years, let alone since the Aga was invented in 1922! The modern cook is encouraged to look for the best seasonal ingredients available and to support farmers' markets and organic growers as well as the chain supermarkets. Healthy, low-fat cooking is easy to achieve with an Aga, as well as cooking for children – something previously overlooked in other Aga books. The recipes, advice and ideas contained in this book will give you confidence and inspiration.

What Aga cooks really want to have are new ideas for everyday cooking, hints and tips to be either more creative or simply make life easier – from cooking poppadums directly on the Boiling Plate to how to open awkward jam jars on the Simmering Plate.

Aga Cooking is to be used as a modern up-to-date bible of cooking on the Aga. Written with the modern Aga cook in mind, this book is certain to demystify cooking on an Aga. Each recipe also gives timings and temperatures for cooking in conventional ovens such as the Aga Six-Four series, Aga Companion and the Aga Module. This means that you can cook your favourite recipes using other ovens, and share them with non-Aga-owning friends.

Amy Willcock

ga food... fast food... easy

HOW IT ALL BEGAN

In 1922 Dr Gustav Dalen, a Swedish physicist and Nobel Prize winner, invented and patented the world's first solid fuel heat storage cooker – now known around the world as the Aga. This soon became a popular method of cooking in larger country houses. The Aga has been through many fuel options, introducing oil and gas and, much later, electric-powered models. The range of Aga colours available is always being updated and added to, but cream – the original colour – still remains the all-time favourite.

In 1996 Aga introduced an electric module fitted to the left side of any fuelled Aga. It is a conventional cooker made in the Aga style and in 1998 the companion was launched, which meant that everyone could have a touch of Aga in their kitchen. At the beginning of the new millennium, Aga produced the new Aga Six-Four series, which combines the cooking style of a range cooker (six-burner gas hot plate and three electric ovens) with the unmistakable appearance of an Aga. Agalinks (www.agalinks.com) is the exciting lifestyle site that can offer expert advice on everything from travel, property and on-line shopping to what to cook for your next dinner party.

AGA KNOW-HOW

The following pages explain how each cooking area of your Aga works and why. Every Aga is unique, whether it is brand new or old and battered. No two Agas are the same. It doesn't matter if they are gas, electric or oil as a burner heats them all in the same way. The heat from the burner unit is transferred to the ovens and hot plates where it is stored. When the insulated lids are down, they hold in the heat. When the lids are up, heat is lost.

All the ovens on the right-hand side of the aga are externally vented, keeping cooking smells out of the kitchen and succulence in the food. The stored heat is released as radiant heat, which is what locks in the flavour and moisture, giving such superb results. Heat lost through cooking is automatically restored. Each Aga is thermostatically controlled, so you can forget

a two-oven AGA

a four-oven AGA

fast food... easy food... a

about exact temperatures. I recommend that new Aga users buy an oven thermometer and hang it in the middle of the ovens first thing in the morning to see what the temperatures are. Do this only once, just to give you an indication of what the oven temperatures are.

The cooking times for older Aga cookers may have to be adjusted, because insulation used then was not as good as it is now. New insulating materials are being developed all the time, so newer Aga models benefit from modern technology.

The heat indicator should be checked first thing in the morning, just to confirm that the Aga is up to heat. The mercury should sit on the black line, which means that the Aga has its full amount of stored heat. Although I do know of Aga cookers where the mercury is in the black and they are fully up to heat, this is a rare occurrence. If it does happen to a newly installed Aga, ask your Aga dealer to check it out. This is where the quirks of the Aga can be so different. It is quite usual for the mercury to drop during cooking – don't worry as the heat will automatically be restored.

I only turn off my Aga for servicing, and once the temperature has been reset and I am happy with the mercury position I don't touch it until the next service (in my case, once a year). After installation or servicing, make a note of the mercury position for the first few mornings, and move the control up or down until the mercury consistently reaches the black central line.

There may be times when you are doing a lot of cooking and need more heat. Before you move the control knob, examine your cooking method. *There is one golden rule in Aga cooking: keep the lids down and cook in the ovens.* Around 80 per cent of cooking should be done in the ovens. The Aga's combustion system, heat path and insulation schemes are designed on this premise. Once you have taken this on board, you will never suffer heat loss again.

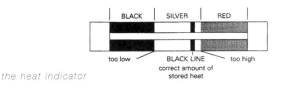

the heat indicator

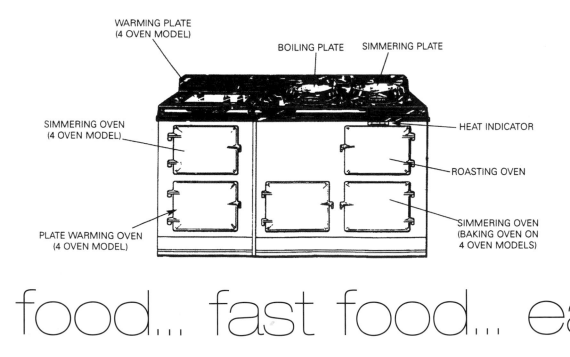

THE BOILING PLATE

The Boiling Plate is situated directly over the burner, making it the hottest plate. It is used when you want a fierce or high heat to bring foods to the boil or for stir-frying. Bread is toasted on it using the Aga Toaster. It is also where the Aga Kettle is brought up to the boil.

THE SIMMERING PLATE

The Simmering Plate gives off a gentle heat ideal for simmering, but the biggest advantage is that you can cook directly on it, like a griddle. Season it just as you would a new frying pan by putting vegetable oil on a piece of kitchen paper and wiping the plate's surface. Do this two or three times, leaving the lid up so that some of the oil burns off and does not leave an oily build-up. If you don't use the plate as a griddle for a while, re-season before use.

To cook on the plate, lift the lid a few minutes before cooking to reduce the heat a little, wipe the surface with a small amount of oil and proceed with cooking. Remember, too much oil makes smoke! I cook pancakes, fried eggs, toasted sandwiches and tortillas like this. I always use the round pre-cut piece of Bake-O-Glide (available from Aga dealers) on the

Simmering Plate. This eliminates the need for seasoning the plate and needs little, if any, oil, giving me a low-fat cooking option.

Always close the lids promptly on both plates when you have finished using them, otherwise precious heat escapes. Each plate takes three large saucepans.

THE WARMING PLATE (4-OVEN AGA ONLY)

The Warming Plate is to the left of the Boiling Plate and is a very useful area to warm things such as awkwardly shaped serving dishes and teapots. It is also great for resting large joints of roasted meat.

THE AGA OVENS

The 2-oven Aga has a Roasting Oven and a Simmering Oven. The 4-oven Aga has a Roasting Oven, a Baking Oven, a Simmering Oven and a Warming Oven. The runners in the ovens are always counted from the top downwards.

The reason foods taste so much better when cooked in an Aga is because they retain valuable moisture, which is usually lost during conventional cooking. This is because in some cases the surface of the food is sealed in by the Aga's unique radiant heat. By and large, the air in a conventional oven is hotter than in an Aga; the hotter the air, the more moisture it will absorb, which can dry food out.

As there are no dials to control the temperatures, food is cooked by position and timing. If you think in those terms, adapting conventional recipes will become second nature. Looking at food while it is cooking is not a problem because the cast iron ovens retain the heat all around the inside of the oven and opening the door will not result in a sudden heat loss.

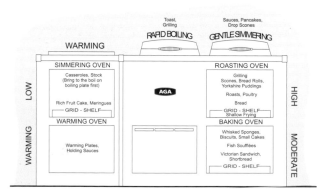

THE ROASTING OVEN

The Roasting Oven is the hottest oven. Think of it as having four different areas of cooking space:

High: top of the oven

Middle: centre of the oven

Low: near the bottom

Floor: the oven floor

What cooks where:

The oven is slightly hotter on the left side, which is near the burner.

High: the top of the oven is perfect for cooking foods that require a very high heat, such as grilled bacon and Yorkshire puddings, or for crisping up the tops of cottage pies or browning meats.

Middle: the middle of the Roasting Oven is where joints of meat are cooked. Timings for roasts cooked here are the same as for conventional cookers. However, some roasts can be started here and then finished off in the Simmering Oven, but timings will be longer. For 2-oven Aga owners, this is the area to use for baking but you will need an item of cookware called an Aga Cake Baker. It is essential for cakes that need more than 40 minutes' baking time. The cake baker is an 'oven within an oven', creating a moderate temperature for a longer amount of time. For cakes requiring less than 40 minutes, using the cold Plain Shelf in the Roasting Oven creates a moderate oven temperature, but only for about 20-30 minutes. Once the plain shelf absorbs the oven's heat, it is useless until it is taken out and cooled. The

Plain Shelf must not be stored in the Aga. It must go into the Aga cold. Four-oven Agas do not require a cake baker as they have a Baking Oven.

To use the cake baker, select the correct-sized tin and remove the trivet and cake tins from inside the cake baker. Put the outer container and lid onto the Roasting Oven floor to heat up. Pour the cake mix into the tin and remove the cake baker from the oven. Set the trivet and cake tin inside the cake baker. Replace the lid and put it on the Roasting Oven floor. Set the timer. Using the cake baker means there is no need to turn cakes round or fear of over-browning.

Low: this is the part of the oven where roast potatoes, bread and sponge cakes are cooked. When making sponge cakes, do not use the cake baker; instead use heavy-based tins and place the grid shelf on the floor of the Roasting Oven and the plain shelf on the second set of runners just above, to cut the heat and create a moderate oven temperature.

Floor: think of the Roasting Oven floor as an extension of the hot plates – anything you can cook on the hot plates you can do on the Roasting Oven floor. Use it to fry foods such as onions or eggs or for browning meats. Heat a frying pan with a little oil in it on the floor of the Roasting Oven; add your ingredients and fry. Do not put wooden or Bakelite-handled pans into the Roasting Oven. A good item of cookware to invest in is the Aga Grill Pan. By heating it up in the Roasting Oven you can 'grill' foods in it. I use this part of the oven the most.

The Aga cake baker

THE BAKING OVEN

This oven is only available with the 4-oven Aga. It is perfect for all baking as it is a moderate oven. It can also be used like the Roasting Oven but with longer cooking times. The top of the oven is slightly hotter.

What cooks where:

Top of the oven: small cakes are cooked to perfection.

Centre: for brownies, muffins, biscuits, breads and crumbles. Also, the right temperature for baking fish.

Bottom: when cooking soufflés or cheesecakes here, they must be off the floor. Slide a grid shelf on to the oven floor and stand the tin or dish on the grid shelf.

THE SIMMERING OVEN

This is the slow oven. On the 2-oven Aga it is on the bottom right; on the 4-oven Aga it is on the top left. On the 2-oven Aga it has three sets of runners; on the 4-oven model there is only one set in the middle. The gentle heat of the Simmering Oven is ideal for slow cooking and cooking overnight. Everything to be cooked in this oven, apart from meringues and a few other recipes, must be started either on the hot plates or in the Roasting Oven and brought up to the boil before going into the Simmering Oven. Saucepans must have tight-fitting flat lids that can be stacked one on top of the other. It is fine to put wooden and Bakelite-handled pans in the Simmering Oven.

What cooks where:

Centre: this is where casseroles, soups and stocks are made. Bring to the boil on the Boiling Plate, then transfer to the Simmering Oven. Roasts such as lamb and pork can be started in the Roasting Oven, then transferred to the Simmering Oven, leaving valuable space in the Roasting Oven for other dishes. Rice puddings and baked custards are also started in the Roasting Oven, then transferred to the Simmering Oven for slow, gentle cooking. The temperature is also just right for steamed puddings.

Bottom: if you don't have a Baking Oven, this is where fruitcakes and meringues are cooked. Pin-head oatmeal can be brought to the boil on the Boiling Plate then placed on a grid shelf on the floor of the oven and left overnight for creamy porridge the next morning. This is the best place for drying fruits and vegetables, such as tomatoes and mushrooms, or infusing oils.

Floor: the floor of the Simmering Oven is perfect for cooking rice and root vegetables. The Aga method of cooking for rice (see page 124) results in delicious fluffy rice, while the Aga method for root vegetables (see page 110) is extremely easy and nutritious. The Aga is perfect for the busy person as it waits for you and there is no fear of ruining or burning foods. If you are delayed, food can wait patiently in the Simmering Oven and still taste great.

THE WARMING OVEN

Available in the 4-oven Aga only, this is primarily a place to keep things warm. As well as reviving the odd orphaned lamb, it is where plates are warmed, and wet shoes stuffed with newspapers are dried out! It can, of course, dry out fruits and vegetables like the Simmering Oven but they will take much longer.

COOKWARE FOR YOUR AGA

Each new Aga comes with the basic Aga kit:

2 grid shelves

1 large roasting tin and grill rack

Half-size roasting tin and grill rack

1 plain shelf

1 toaster

1 wire brush

I would suggest 2-oven Aga owners invest in another plain shelf if you like to do a lot of baking, and I recommend that 2- and 4-oven Aga owners invest in a few more half-size roasting tins.

My Aga batterie de cuisine consists of:
1 x 9 litre stainless steel stockpot *
2 x 1.5 litre stainless steel shallow casserole dish *
2 x 2.7 litre stainless steel sauté casserole dish *
2 x 1.25 litre stainless steel shallow saucepan *
1 x milk pan *
1 x cake baker* (2-oven Aga owners only)
2 x half-size hard anodised shallow baking tray (fits directly onto the runners) *
2 x full-size hard anodised baking tray (fits directly onto the runners and can be used as a plain shelf)
1 x cast iron grill pan *
1 x 1.5 litre hard anodised kettle *
1 x 3.5 litre aluminium interior non-stick coated kettle
1 x cast iron sauté pan
2 x 18 cm loose-bottomed hard anodised sponge tins *
2 x 20 cm loose-bottomed hard anodised sponge tins *
1 x 28 cm diameter sauté pan with glass lid and removable handle for use in the ovens *

1 x hard anodised turkey roasting tin
1 x pizza peel (very useful for getting tarts out of the oven) *

Don't be alarmed at the size of my list – many pans have been collected over the years and do not need to be bought all at once. I have marked the items I think are essential with an asterisk.

Saucepans, Tins and Casseroles

One of the first things new Aga owners want to know is whether they have to buy new saucepans. The easy answer is no, because most people will have some suitable cookware already. However, to maximise the Aga, use the Aga range of saucepans. They have machined-flat, heavy ground bases and are able to reach boiling point very quickly, thereby conserving heat. Pans that are not suitable waste valuable heat time and energy and there will be a marked difference in cooking times. Cast iron, earthenware, ceramic and copper are all suitable for the Aga. Glass Pyrex can also be used in the ovens on the grid shelves.

To test if your existing saucepans are suitable for the Aga, fill each one with cold water and put it on the Boiling Plate. Hold either side of the pan down and see if it rocks. If the pan is flat, tiny bubbles appear uniformly over the bottom of the surface. It is not flat if the bubbles appear only in certain areas of the pan.

Saucepans with wooden or Bakelite handles are not suitable for the Roasting Oven. Buy pans that are fully ovenproof and that can be used anywhere on the Aga. Saucepans and casseroles should be as wide as possible so that they cover most of the hot plate surface. The flat lids on Aga pans enable stacking in the ovens, giving masses of room for cooking.

Baking and Cooking Tins

When buying tins for the Aga, make sure that they slide onto the runners. This will mean the full capacity of the ovens will be realised. The one tin that I use constantly is the half-size shallow hard anodised baking tray. The full-size one can also be used as a plain shelf. They are sufficiently heavy duty to use on the hot plates and ideal for things like roasting potatoes. Make sure muffin and other specialised tins are also as heavy duty as possible. Cake tins must be heavy duty. As dark colours absorb heat more quickly than lighter ones, you may find in some cases a darker cake tin will require a slightly shorter cooking time than, say, a lighter aluminium cake tin.

Kettles

To get the best from your kettle, buy a size that suits your needs. There is no point in getting the 2-litre kettle if your household only has 2 people in it. A common complaint about kettles is that they become pitted at the bottom and can take a long time to come to the boil.

The first problem occurs when boiled water is not fully used and the water level is just topped up. This is bad practice as the boiled water leaves mineral deposits sitting on the bottom of the kettle which cause pitting. When this happens, it takes longer to bring water up to the boil and the kettle is less efficient. Using a smaller kettle ensures you empty the water when making pots of tea and that the kettle is always filled with fresh water. If you are using a large kettle, only fill it with the amount of water needed for the job. If you live in a hard-water area, it is essential to clean the kettle once a week.

Bake-O-Glide

This is a lifesaver. Use it to line tins, making cleaning a cinch, or on the Simmering Plate. It is dishwasher-safe and only small amounts of fat are needed, if at all, to make surfaces non-stick. Roast potatoes crisp up beautifully and the crunchy bits left in the tin lift off easily. I use the pre-cut circle on the Simmering Plate to fry eggs, cook pancakes and make toasted sandwiches.

CLEANING AND CARING FOR YOUR AGA

The best way to have a clean Aga is to avoid getting it dirty in the first place. If you use the ovens for cooking foods that splatter (frying and grilling), the hot plates will stay clean. Pushing pans to the rear of the oven will keep the aluminium door clean as well. Keep a damp cloth at the ready to wipe up spills as they happen. Acidic liquids and milk can cause pitting to the enamel top. Don't drag pans across the top or the surface will eventually scratch.

Cleaning the Ovens

Oven cleaning doesn't really exist with an Aga. The ovens self-clean because the constant high heat means that food spills carbonise and only need to

be brushed out with the wire brush. (If you have a metal nozzle on your vacuum cleaner, you can suck out the carbonised bits with it.) The Aga doors must NEVER be immersed in water as this would destroy the insulation.

To clean the doors, simply lay out a double thickness of tea towels on a flat surface and then carefully lift off the doors from the hinges. Use gauntlets to move the doors, as they will be very hot. Lay the doors on the tea towels enamel side down and leave to cool for a few minutes. Using a damp wire wool scouring pad and a little washing-up liquid, firmly go over the inside of the door – it will scratch the aluminium but it won't harm it. Wipe it clean and replace the doors on the hinges.

To clean the outside of the oven doors and the enamelled front and top, use a proprietary mild cream cleaner. Lightly apply it with a damp cloth, then wipe with a dry cloth to polish off any residue. A silicone polish can also be used on the front and top of the cooker to help control the dust. This is a good idea for darker-coloured cookers, where the dust tends to be more visible.

Cleaning the Hot Plates

Clean the hot plate surfaces with the wire brush. Food will burn off and all that is needed is to clear away any carbonised bits that will interfere with the contact between saucepan bottoms and the hot surface. It is a good idea to keep the wire brush handy when making toast so that you can clear away any breadcrumbs immediately.

To clean the inside of the Simmering Plate lid (the Boiling Plate lid rarely needs cleaning as the intense heat keeps it clean), lift the lid and leave open for a few minutes to cool slightly, then place a grid shelf over the hot plate and the plain self on top of the grid shelf. This will reduce the heat, allowing easier cleaning in the middle of the lid, and is also a safety precaution in case your hand slips. Use a soapy wire wool pad and a damp cloth. The inside of the lid will scratch but it will not affect the cooker's performance.

Clean the chromium lids with a soapy damp cloth and buff with a clean dry tea towel. Do not use wire wool or any harsh abrasives on the chrome. To avoid the tops of the lids being scratched, either use the specially designed round Aga oven pads or a folded tea towel to protect them if you place dishes on top. Don't put heavy pans or tins on them as this may dent them.

SERVICING YOUR AGA

Always use an authorised Aga distributor to service your Aga. If you have moved into a house with an Aga, try to find out its service history and the telephone number and contact name of the company that services it. Gas and electric Aga cookers should be serviced once a year and oil-fuelled Aga cookers every six months. The standard check and service will take about an hour.

The night before a service, remember to turn off your Aga so that it cools down. Turn the burner off and leave the pilot on (refer to the inside of the burner compartment door). After servicing, the Aga technician will re-light the Aga for you.

If you have friends staying or even members of the family, try to make them 'Aga Aware' so that scratches, spills and dents are avoided.

ja food... fast food... easy

HIDDEN EXTRAS

The Aga is not just a wonderful cooker, it also has hidden talents and can sometimes act like an extra pair of hands. One of the best things about the cooker is its ability to do the ironing! The Aga will become the focal point of the kitchen and bottoms will have to be prised off the chrome rail!

Aga 'Ironing'

To 'iron' items such as sheets, hankies, tea towels, vests, pillow cases and so on, fold the newly washed and spun laundry. Smooth and press in creases firmly by hand and place them on the Simmering Plate lid. Turn them over when one side is dry. Take care not to drape washing over the handles of the lids and do not obstruct the air vents on the burner door when hanging sheets on the chrome rail. Press sheets by hanging them over the chrome rail, then fold and press firmly when almost dry and transfer to the lid of the Simmering Plate to press. Never place laundry on the Boiling Plate lid as it may become scorched.

Hints and Tips

● Buy two really reliable and accurate timers, preferably digital. Timers are crucial to the Aga cook. Or buy a timer on a long cord so that you can wear it around your neck – this means you will hear the timer wherever you are.

● Tie a red ribbon around the rail or above so that it catches your eye and reminds you something is in the oven. A magnet with a note attached works well too.

● Dry awkward gadgets such as graters and garlic crushers at the back of the Aga and they will dry in all those hard to reach places.

● Dry glassware and decanters on a tea towel at the back of the Aga.

● Keep your wooden spoons near the Aga as it will keep them dry.

● Heat unusual-shaped dishes at the back of the Aga. To warm large platters, place a tea towel underneath them to stop slipping and stand them upright propped against the back or side of the Aga.

● Always pre-heat the Aga toaster to prevent bread sticking to it.

● To save time and energy, pre-heat pans in the Roasting Oven (do not put in saucepans with wooden or plastic handles).

● Protect open lids from splatters with a tea towel draped over the back (remove before closing the lid).

● Opening new jar lids could not be simpler. Invert the jar top onto the Simmering Plate for a few seconds and you will hear it release. Protect your hands with a tea towel before touching the metal lid.

● Poppadums can be cooked directly on the Boiling Plate with the lid down; they are ready in seconds.

● Cook pancakes, drop scones, fried eggs and toasted cheese sandwiches directly on the Simmering Plate.

● A lot of food can be cooked in advance and reheated when ready to serve. For example, roast potatoes can be roasted for 20 minutes, then taken out, left overnight in a cool area, then blasted in the Roasting Oven for 20 minutes when ready to eat (see page 111). Yorkshire pudding can be done in the morning when the Roasting Oven is at its hottest, then reheated for 8 minutes before serving (see page 189).

● Clean crusty pans in a biological washing powder solution by whisking the powder into some hot water to dissolve, then soak pan overnight.

fast food... easy food... a

● Keep salt in a salt box next to the Aga and it will remain dry.

● Use all of the black surface area on the top of the Aga – it is great for melting butter or chocolate. Break up the chocolate into pieces, put it into a bowl and stand it to the left of the Boiling Plate and it will melt in no time at all. Warm flour and sugar for baking here as well.

● For 2-oven Aga owners, plan to do your baking when the ovens will be cooler, such as after a heavy cooking session.

● Stuff wet shoes or boots with newspaper and leave to dry near the Aga, or if you have a 4-oven Aga, use the Warming Oven.

● Seal milky flower stems on the Boiling Plate.

CONVERTING RECIPES

Converting conventional recipes is easy. As all Aga cooking is done by timing and position, just remember how the heat is distributed in each oven and once you decide where the food is to be cooked, adjust the timings accordingly. I tend to underestimate the time by roughly 10 minutes, as I can always put the dish back in for a little longer if necessary. Use the recipes in this book as a point of reference when converting conventional recipes.

Example:

Let's take a muffin recipe. The ingredients and method are exactly the same. The recipe calls for a pre-heated oven, and a temperature of 180°C/350°F/gas 4; time for cooking is 40-45 minutes.

For a 2-oven Aga:

There is no need to pre-heat the oven as the Aga is always ready to cook. Make the batter according to the recipe, and pour the mix into the muffin tin.

I would use the lower/bottom half of the Roasting Oven, but not the Roasting Oven floor. Place the grid shelf on the floor of the Roasting Oven and the cold plain shelf (to make a moderate oven temperature 180°C/350°F/gas 4) on the second set of runners. Estimate the time at 30 minutes, but it may take up to 45 minutes if the oven is not right up to temperature. Have a look at them throughout the cooking time and check after about 25 minutes. They are done when pale golden and shrinking away from the sides of the tin.

For a 4-oven Aga:

As above but cook in the Baking Oven omitting the cold plain shelf until it is needed (probably 20-25 minutes into the cooking time).

Aga Temperatures
Roasting Oven Hot
      Approx. 240-260°C 475-500°F gas 8-9
Baking Oven Moderate
      Approx. 180-200°C 350-400°F gas 4-6
Simmering Oven Slow
      Approx. 150-135°C 225-275°F gas 1
Warming Oven Warm
      Approx. 70-90°C 150-200°F gas ¼
These represent typical centre-oven temperatures

Mercury Position
Line in black area: less heat is stored so cooking will take longer, temperature too low.
Line in red area: more than required amount of heat stored, temperature too high.

THE AGA WAY OF COOKING

There is one question that crops up at every workshop or demonstration I do: "I will be halfway through cooking Sunday Lunch and find I run out of heat when it comes to cooking the roast potatoes and or Yorkshire pudding. The mercury zooms down on the thermometer. How can I prevent heat loss?"

The answer is to examine your method of cooking. Heat loss often occurs if you use the hot plates too much beforehand. Perhaps you cooked breakfast on top rather than in the ovens that morning? Or par-boiled potatoes on the Boiling Plate instead of in the Simmering Oven. Check how much the lids are up.

If you are still experiencing problems after satisfying yourself that you are doing everything correctly, you are probably not planning your cooking timetable for the menu you have chosen. Yorkshire pudding can be cooked first thing in the morning when the ovens are at their hottest and successfully re-heated just before serving. Roast potatoes can be cooked up to their final 20 minutes the day before. And even green vegetables can be blanched the day before, ready to be re-heated the next day just before serving. Good cooking, whether it is on an Aga or conventional cooker, is all about planning and preparation.

PLANNING AND PREPARATION

Make full use of the ovens by planning your oven space. An easy way of doing this is to use the plain shelf. Put the shelf on your work surface and arrange the pieces of cookware you need to use on top of it or put the empty cookware you plan to use inside the oven. Take into account grid shelves and, if you can, stack pots and pans. Aga pots and pans are made with flat lids for this reason, but if you are using conventional saucepans, invert the lids if possible and carry on stacking (but check that the lids will be safe and not fall in). When stacking pans, always point the handles in the same direction and use tins that fit directly on to the runners for maximum oven capacity.

When you fill the Warming or Simmering Ovens, try to put the foods you are serving first at the front.

Try to plan your menu around your Aga. Consider logistics. Invariably food moves around the Aga, usually ending in the Warming or Simmering Ovens, on the Warming Plate or on protected hot plate lids. Plan to use the space they leave in the ovens well. You may find that you cook food in a different order than usual as the safety net of the Simmering or Warming Ovens allows for greater flexibility. Plan in which order to cook the recipes. Decide which recipes can be cooked ahead and take into account thawing times and re-heating times if applicable. Serve some foods that can be completely done ahead and just need re-heating.

AGA CAN DO CONVENIENCE FOOD TOO!

The everyday reality for many of us is that dinner is just as likely to come out of a packet as it is from the latest cook book. This is where the Aga comes in – forget the microwave, just pop the foil packet on a baking tray and slide it on to the third or fourth set of runners in the Roasting Oven and dinner is ready in no time at all. Because the Aga is on 24 hours a day, there is no waiting for ovens to heat up. So even before you take off your coat, take out a store-bought lasagne and garlic bread from the freezer and cook it in the same time it takes to hang up your coat, kick off your shoes, pour a glass of wine and kiss the children good night!

Aga A.A.G. (At A Glance)

Below are some helpful general cooking positions and, in my experience, 20 minutes seems to be the magic amount of time for many dishes.

TECHNIQUES

Grilling: use the Aga grill pan on the Roasting Oven floor or on the Boiling Plate.

Frying: use the Roasting Oven floor and first set of runners in the Roasting Oven.

Roasting: Roasting, Baking and Simmering Ovens – use Roasting Oven for conventional timings; Baking and/or Simmering Ovens for slow roasting.

Browning Meat: use the first set of runners in the Roasting Oven, then move to the Roasting Oven floor.

Steaming: start on the Boiling Plate or in the Roasting Oven, cover, then move to the Simmering Oven.

Boiling: Boiling Plate. Once boil is established, move to the Roasting Oven floor.

Simmering: start on the Boiling Plate, cover with a lid, then move to the Simmering Oven. To reduce liquids, remove lid and continue in the Simmering Oven.

Poaching: bring to the boil on the Boiling Plate, then move to the Roasting or Simmering Oven depending on food being poached (poach eggs on the Simmering Plate).

Braising: bring up to the boil on the Boiling Plate for 5-10 minutes, then move to the Simmering or Baking Oven.

FOODS

Jacket potatoes: third set of runners or floor of the Roasting Oven.

Roasted vegetables: first set of runners or floor of the Roasting Oven.

Frozen pizza: directly on the Roasting Oven floor.

Rice: bring up to the boil on the Boiling Plate, cover, then transfer to the Simmering Oven. In general, most quantities of rice (unless very large) take about 20 minutes.

Pasta: boil on the Boiling Plate.

Cookies and biscuits: fourth set of runners with the Cold Plain Shelf on the second set of runners in the Roasting Oven. Third set of runners in the Baking Oven.

Muffins: grid shelf on floor of Roasting Oven with Cold Plain Shelf above, or on fourth set of runners with Cold Plain Shelf on second set of runners. In Baking Oven on third set of runners.

Bread: directly on the Roasting Oven floor.

Frozen breads: third set of runners in the Roasting Oven for 10-15 minutes, covered with foil if browning too much.

Toasted sandwiches: use the round Bake-O-Glide and cook directly on the Simmering Plate.

Cheesecake: grid shelf on the floor of Roasting Oven with Cold Plain Shelf on just above for 5-10 minutes or until just set, then move to the Simmering Oven for 35-45 minutes.

Frozen fish fingers/chicken nuggets/chips: start on the Roasting Oven floor, then move to third set of runners (total cooking time about 10-12 minutes).

Crispy bacon: use Bake-O-Glide in a shallow baking tray on the Roasting Oven floor.

Melting chocolate/butter: at the back of the black enamel top, on the Warming Plate or in the Simmering Oven.

breakfast
and brunch

the full aga breakfast

I find that a proper breakfast can be one of the hardest meals to get absolutely right – everything must be cooked to order, usually for large numbers of people. You'll be familiar with the scene – Sunday morning and the household drifts down in dribs and drabs, all looking forward to a cooked breakfast! Co-ordinating toast, eggs, bacon and so on can become a nightmare, but not for the Aga owner!

per person:

1 or 2 eggs	1 large field mushroom
2 rashers bacon	half a tomato
1 sausage	toast

1 Depending on how many you are cooking for, use either the half-size Aga roasting tin or the full-size one. Line it with Bake-O-Glide, and put the mushrooms and tomato halves, cut side up, on the bottom of the tin. Drizzle over a little oil and season with salt and pepper. Place the grill rack on top of them and put the sausages on the rack over the mushrooms and tomatoes (do not prick the sausages).

2 Slide the tin on to the first set of runners in the ROASTING OVEN, and cook for 10 minutes. When the timer goes off, take the tin out of the oven, turn the sausages and lay the bacon rashers on the grill rack. Pop it back into the ROASTING OVEN for a further 10 minutes. Depending on the thickness of the bacon and the size of the sausages, you may need to adjust the timings.

3 When everything is cooked, take the tin out of the oven and put the bacon, sausages, tomatoes and mushrooms on to a warmed platter, cover with foil and transfer to the SIMMERING OVEN to keep warm while you cook the eggs. If you want well-done bacon, after you remove the sausages, tomatoes and mushrooms to the platter, take off the grill rack and put the bacon on the bottom of the tin. Place the tin on the floor of the ROASTING OVEN and let the bacon cook to your liking.

4 If you want to make fried bread as well, do it in exactly the same way as for well-done bacon, adding a little more oil to the tin if necessary. It will take about 5 minutes for each side.

5 There are two ways of cooking fried eggs – either in the Aga or on the Aga.

In the Aga: When you remove the sausages, bacon and so on from the tin, add a little more oil to the tin and put it on the ROASTING OVEN floor to get really hot. When the oil is hot, crack the eggs into the tin one at a time. The large tin will take about 6 large eggs and the half-size tin about 3 large eggs. Baste the eggs with the fat and put the tin back into the oven for 3 minutes or until they are done to your liking.

On the Aga: Open the SIMMERING PLATE lid and either grease it with a little oil, or use a round pre-cut circle of Bake-O-Glide and put it directly onto the SIMMERING PLATE surface. Drizzle a little oil on to a piece of kitchen paper and rub it over the plate. Crack the egg on to the hot surface and close the lid. The egg will cook in about 2 minutes. The SIMMERING PLATE surface can take about 3 large eggs at a time. (If you have an older Aga with a dented lid, check to see whether it touches the top of the egg when you close it. If it does, leave the lid open. The egg will take a little longer to cook.)

6 To make the toast, put a slice of bread in the Aga toasting rack and place it on the BOILING PLATE. Close the lid but keep an eye on it as it will toast very quickly; turn over to do the other side. To stop very fresh bread from sticking to the toaster, heat the rack first on the BOILING PLATE before inserting the bread. If you like crispy toast, leave the BOILING PLATE lid open.

roasting coffee beans

To roast your own green coffee beans, spread the beans out in the large roasting tin and hang the tin on the first set of runners of the ROASTING OVEN for 25-30 minutes or until the oils start to run and they turn golden brown. Shake the pan three or four times during cooking to roast evenly.

aga kippers

Put the kippers in an Aga roasting tin. Add about a tablespoon of water to the bottom of the tin and place a knob of butter on each kipper. Cover with foil and cook in the ROASTING OVEN for 15-20 minutes.

Conventional Cooking:
Pre heat the oven to 220°C/425°F/gas 7 and cook as above, in the centre of the oven.

aga porridge

serves 1

75 g pinhead oatmeal
600 ml water

brown sugar and cream, to serve

1 Put the oatmeal and water in an Aga pan and bring to the boil on the BOILING PLATE. Transfer to the SIMMERING PLATE and simmer for 2 minutes.
2 Meanwhile, put the grid shelf on the floor of the SIMMERING OVEN. Cover the pan with the lid and put the grid shelf on the floor of the SIMMERING OVEN. Leave overnight. Stir before serving and add brown sugar and cream.

Variation:
If using normal rolled oats, put them in a pan with the measured amount of water and leave covered on the black enamelled top at the back of the Aga overnight. Serve with brown sugar and cream.

Conventional Cooking:
Follow the instructions on the packet.

popovers with fruit compote

makes 6

vegetable oil, for coating the tin	300 ml milk
175 g plain flour	1 tbsp vegetable oil
½ tsp salt	2 tbsp fruit compote of your choice
freshly grated nutmeg	icing sugar, to dust
3 eggs, beaten	crème fraîche or cream, to serve

1 Lightly grease a 6-cup muffin tin and pre-heat it in the ROASTING OVEN for 5 minutes.

2 Sift the flour into a bowl. Add the salt, nutmeg, eggs, milk and vegetable oil and mix well so there are no lumps.

3 Ladle the mixture into the tin and place a teaspoon of fruit compote into each cup. Cook in the ROASTING OVEN for 10-15 minutes or until golden and risen.

4 Remove from the tin, dust with icing sugar and serve straight away with crème fraîche or cream.

Conventional Cooking:

Pre-heat the oven to 220°C/425°F/gas 7 and prepare as above. Cook the popovers in the centre of the oven for 12 minutes or until golden and risen.

banana and walnut muffins

makes 12

3 large bananas, mashed	2 tsp baking powder
3 large eggs, slightly beaten	1 tsp baking soda
580 g plain flour	pinch of salt
120 ml vegetable oil	200 g chopped walnuts
270 g golden caster sugar	200 g muesli

1 Line a 12-hole muffin tin with muffin papers and set aside. In a large bowl, mix together all of the ingredients thoroughly. Spoon the mix into the muffin tin, filling the papers to the top.

2 Put the grid shelf on the floor of the ROASTING OVEN and put in the muffin tin. Slide the cold PLAIN SHELF on to the third set of runners and bake for 20-25 minutes or until golden. To test if they are cooked in the middle, insert the point of a knife or a skewer; if it comes out clean, they are ready. If the mix is still loose, put them back in the oven for a few minutes. Remove the muffins from the tin and cool on a wire rack. For a 4-oven Aga, place the muffin tin on the fourth set of runners in the BAKING OVEN and cook for 25 minutes.

Conventional Cooking:

Pre-heat the oven to 200°C/400°F/gas 6 and bake the muffins for 20-25 minutes.

right: popovers with fruit compote

toasted bagel with smoked salmon, poached egg and hollandaise sauce

per person:

1 egg	**FOR THE HOLLANDAISE SAUCE:**
½ bagel	2 large egg yolks
a little butter	juice of ½ a lemon
2 slices of smoked salmon	1 tbsp water
1 tbsp hollandaise sauce (see below)	pinch of caster sugar
black pepper	salt and white pepper
a few snipped chives	250 g unsalted butter, cut into cubes

1 First make the hollandaise sauce. Place the egg yolks, lemon juice, water, sugar, salt and pepper in a bowl over a pan of simmering water on the SIMMERING PLATE (do not let the bowl come into contact with the water) and whisk until the mix leaves a ribbon trail. Whisking constantly, drop in the cubes of butter one at a time – don't drop in the next cube until the previous one has been absorbed; this will take some time. When you have a thick, velvety sauce, taste for seasoning, then set aside until ready to serve.

Conventional Cooking:
Bring the bowl of water to the simmer over a medium heat and proceed as above.

2 Put a saucepan full of water on the SIMMERING PLATE. When it has reached a gentle simmer, crack the egg into the water and poach for about 2 minutes.

Conventional Cooking:
Bring water to a simmer over a medium heat and proceed as above.

3 While the egg is cooking, use the Aga toaster to toast the bagel. Spread the toasted bagel with a little butter and top with the smoked salmon. When the egg is ready, lift out the egg with a slotted spoon and rest the spoon on a piece of kitchen paper to drain. Place the egg on top of the smoked salmon and spoon over some hollandaise sauce. Season with black pepper and a few chives.

aga yoghurt

makes approximately 950 ml

2 litres full fat milk	150 ml live organic yoghurt
300 ml double cream	

1 Bring the milk to the boil in a saucepan on the BOILING PLATE, then simmer on the SIMMERING PLATE until it is reduced by a third.

2 Transfer the warm milk to a clean ceramic or stainless steel bowl and add the cream. Stir well. Cool to blood temperature, then add the yoghurt. Cover the bowl with cling film, then put it on the SIMMERING PLATE lid (protect the lid with a tea towel) and leave the yoghurt overnight to set. It will keep in the refrigerator for about 5 days.

poached apricots and figs with honey and cinnamon

serves 4-6

350 g dried apricots	**1 cinnamon stick**
350 g dried figs	**2 tbsp honey**

1 Place the apricots and figs in an Aga saucepan; add the cinnamon stick and honey. Add just enough water to cover the fruit and cover with a lid.

2 Place on the BOILING PLATE and bring to the boil. Transfer to the SIMMERING OVEN for 2-3 hours or until soft and plump. Serve hot or cold with Aga yoghurt.

Conventional Cooking:
Pre-heat the oven to 150°C/300°F/gas 2. Bring the fruit to the boil, then transfer to the oven and cook for 1-2 hours or until soft and plump.

aga French toast

There are two methods for French toast. The first method is to cook it on the Simmering Plate as for pancakes (see page 28) the second is to cook it in the Roasting Oven. For smaller numbers I would choose the Simmering Plate, but for large numbers the large Aga roasting tin holds about 6 slices of bread.

for 2 slices of bread:

1 tbsp clarified butter (see below)	**vanilla extract**
1 large egg	**2 slices cinnamon and raisin bread**

1 Pour the clarified butter into an Aga roasting tin and put it on the SIMMERING PLATE to heat up.

2 In a flat dish, beat together the egg and a dash of vanilla extract and dip in the bread slices. Put the eggy bread into the tin and place the tin on the ROASTING OVEN floor for 3-4 minutes, then turn over and cook for a further 4 minutes. Serve immediately with sieved icing sugar, strawberry jam and clotted cream.

Conventional Cooking:
Melt a little clarified butter in a frying pan on the hob and cook as above.

Clarified Butter
Place a pack of unsalted butter in a saucepan and cover with a lid. Put it in the SIMMERING OVEN or WARMING OVEN (which will take longer) and leave until it has melted. When melted, pour the butter into a jar or ramekin, leaving the milky residue at the bottom of the pan behind. The clarified butter may be stored for up to 6 months in the refrigerator. Clarified butter has a higher burning point than ordinary butter.

bacon fritters with maple syrup

serves 4

1 tbsp groundnut oil	1 tbsp maple syrup
150 g maple-cured bacon, cut into small cubes	a twist of black pepper
2 large eggs, separated	15 g unsalted butter
30 g plain flour	

1 Heat the oil in a frying pan on the BOILING PLATE and fry the bacon cubes until crispy. Drain them on kitchen paper and set aside.

2 Put the egg yolks, flour, syrup and a twist of pepper into a bowl and mix together thoroughly. Stir in the bacon. Beat the egg whites until stiff and fold them into the bacon mix.

3 Put a round piece of Bake-O-Glide on the SIMMERING PLATE and grease with a little butter. Drop a heaped tablespoon of the batter at a time on to the SIMMERING PLATE and cook until it bubbles around the edges, then turn over with a spatula and cook for a further minute. Serve immediately.

Conventional Cooking:

Use a frying pan over a medium heat to cook bacon. Do not drain all the fat from the frying pan and use the same frying pan to cook the fritters as above.

pancakes

serves 4

240 g plain flour	237 ml buttermilk
1 tbsp caster sugar	30 ml sunflower oil
1 tsp baking powder	1 tsp vanilla extract
½ tsp baking soda	a little extra oil, for greasing Simmering Plate
a pinch of salt	honey or maple syrup and butter, to serve
1 whole large egg	

1 Put all of the ingredients into a bowl and mix really well with a whisk so there are no lumps.

2 Place a round piece of Bake-O-Glide on the SIMMERING PLATE and grease with a little oil. Cooking the pancakes in batches, drop a tablespoon of the pancake mix onto the hot surface and cook until it starts to bubble. Flip the pancake over and cook for 2 minutes or until puffed up. Serve straight away with honey or maple syrup and butter.

Conventional Cooking:

Heat a little of the oil in a frying pan over a medium heat, drop a tablespoon of the pancake batter in and cook in batches as above.

right: bacon fritters with maple syrup

soups
and starters

Soups are easy for the cook and especially delicious when you use your own Aga-made stock which couldn't be easier. The starter recipes are extremely versatile as they can be served as a main dish for lunch just by increasing the amounts.

aga stock

This is the basic method for making Aga stock.

1 Roast off the meat bones in the ROASTING OVEN for about 45 minutes or until brown. Then put them into a stockpot or large pot and cover with cold water. Add herbs, seasoning, a halved onion, a chopped up carrot, celery, garlic and anything else you feel like adding (but not starch-based vegetables such as potatoes).
2 Bring to the boil on the BOILING PLATE and boil rapidly for 5-10 minutes. Cover with a lid and transfer to the SIMMERING OVEN for at least 6 hours or overnight.
3 Skim off the fat and strain through a sieve. Store in the fridge for up to a week, bringing it to the boil before using, or freeze for up to 3 months.

For Chicken and Game Stock:
Use a whole carcass, but do not brown. Start it in cold water.

For Fish Stock:
Do not brown the fish bones, and only cook for about an hour. Keep for 3 days in the fridge.

roasted vine tomato soup

This soup can be frozen and will sit in the SIMMERING OVEN quite happily for a few hours.

serves 6

1 kg vine-ripened tomatoes	1 handful fresh basil leaves, torn
3 large fat garlic cloves, unpeeled	1 heaped tbsp fresh oregano leaves, chopped
1 tbsp olive oil	950 ml vegetable stock
1 tbsp aged balsamic vinegar	salt and pepper

1 Put the tomatoes and garlic cloves into the Aga roasting tin and drizzle with the oil. Season with salt, pepper and balsamic vinegar, half of the basil and the oregano.
2 Slide the tin onto the second set of runners in the ROASTING OVEN and cook for about 30 minutes or until the tomatoes and garlic are soft.
3 Squeeze the skin of the garlic cloves to extract the pulpy flesh into a saucepan. Pour the tomatoes into a sieve and catch the juice in the saucepan. (If you don't mind the tomato skins, don't bother to do this.)

4 Pour the stock into the saucepan and bring to the boil on the BOILING PLATE. Taste for seasoning. Ladle into warm bowls and sprinkle with the rest of the basil and drizzle in some olive oil. Serve with extra balsamic vinegar and ciabatta bread.

Conventional Cooking:
Pre-heat the oven to 150°C/300°F/gas 2. Roast the tomatoes in the middle of the oven for 35-40 minutes. Cook the soup over a medium heat on the hob.

sweetcorn and cheese chowder

serves 6-8

200 g pancetta, cubed	700 g potatoes, peeled and cut into 3 cm cubes
30 g butter	500 g frozen sweetcorn
30 ml olive oil	230 ml whipping cream
2 large onions, peeled and finely chopped	250 g medium Cheddar cheese, grated
50 g plain flour	1 small bag organic tortilla chips, crushed
1.4 litres chicken stock	Salt and pepper

1 Cook the pancetta cubes on the SIMMERING PLATE until crispy, using a saucepan large enough to hold all of the ingredients (a stockpot that fits into the ovens would be perfect).

2 Remove the crispy pancetta and set aside. Pour in the butter and oil, add the chopped onions and cook until they are soft. (If the pot will fit into the ROASTING OVEN, soften the onions there.)

3 Stir the flour into the fat and season with salt and pepper. Cook for about 3 minutes on the SIMMERING PLATE. Stirring all the time, add the stock and potatoes.

Bring up to the boil and transfer to the SIMMERING OVEN for 20 minutes or until the potatoes are tender but still holding their shape.

4 Take the pot out of the oven and add the sweetcorn, whipping cream and three-quarters of the cheese. Bring it back to a gentle simmer and taste for seasoning. Ladle into warmed soup bowls and sprinkle over some crushed tortilla chips, the pancetta and the remaining cheese.

Conventional Cooking:
Cook on the hob for 20-30 minutes over a medium heat.

pancetta and chestnut soup

serves 4

2 tbsp light olive oil	435 g tin chestnut purée
2 tbsp butter	300 ml chicken stock
100 g pancetta, chopped	300 ml double cream
2 large onions, peeled and finely chopped	salt and pepper

1 Heat the oil and butter in a large casserole on the SIMMERING PLATE and fry the pancetta pieces until the fat begins to run. Remove the pancetta and set aside. Add the onion to the fat in the pan and cook until very soft but not coloured. You can do this either on the SIMMERING PLATE or in the ROASTING OVEN.

2 When the onions are soft, add the rest of the ingredients and bring the soup just up to the boil on the

BOILING PLATE. Add most of the pancetta and simmer for a few minutes. Taste for seasoning. (The soup can be liquidised for easier pouring into thermos flasks at this stage if you wish.) Add the reserved pancetta as a garnish when you are ready to serve.

Conventional Cooking:
Cook the soup on the hob over a medium heat as above.

butternut squash and ginger soup with Parmesan croûtons

serves 6

1.5 kg butternut squash

3 tbsp olive oil

1 leek, sliced thinly

2 garlic cloves, crushed

1 parsnip, peeled and chopped

4 cm piece fresh ginger or more to taste, peeled and grated

1 litre vegetable or chicken stock

salt and pepper

FOR THE CROÛTONS:

1 stale loaf of ciabatta bread, cut into bite-sized pieces

1 tbsp olive oil

Parmesan curls, to garnish (shave curls off a hunk of Parmesan cheese using a potato peeler, allowing 1-3 curls per person)

1 Cut the butternut squash in half. Remove the seeds and any fibres, then slice the halves into quarters. Brush the cut edges of the squash with a tablespoon of the olive oil and sprinkle over some salt and pepper. Roast in a roasting tin on the first or second set of runners in the ROASTING OVEN for about 20 minutes or until the squash is soft and slightly charred around the edges. Set aside to cool, then scrape away the flesh from the skin and reserve.

2 While the squash is cooking, heat the remaining oil in a deep pan on the SIMMERING PLATE. Gently cook the leek and garlic until soft. Add the parsnip and ginger. Pour in the stock, bring everything to the boil on the BOILING PLATE and cook for about 3-5 minutes, then transfer to the SIMMERING OVEN for 10 minutes or until the parsnip is tender.

3 To make the croûtons, cut the bread into 2 cm cubes. Toss them in a bowl with the olive oil, making sure they are well coated. Spread on a baking sheet and bake on the first set of runners in the ROASTING OVEN for 8-10 minutes. Watch them carefully as they burn very easily. Leave to cool on a plate lined with kitchen towel.

4 When it is ready, add the roasted butternut squash to the soup and add salt and pepper as needed. Use a food processor to purée the soup, then return it to the pan until warmed through. Serve with the croûtons and garnish with the Parmesan curls.

Conventional Cooking:

Cook the soup on the hob over a medium heat. To bake the croûtons, pre-heat the oven to 200°/400°F/gas 6 and continue as above.

courgette soup

serves 6

1.5 kg courgettes, chopped
1 garlic clove, peeled
1 litre stock
1 tbsp finely chopped mint

1 tbsp torn basil
2 tbsp crème fraîche
50 g Parmesan, grated
salt and pepper

1 Soften the courgettes in the olive oil for about 20 minutes in a frying pan on the floor of the ROASTING OVEN, adding the garlic halfway through the cooking.

2 Remove the pan from the oven, add the stock and season with salt and pepper. Bring up to the simmer on the SIMMERING PLATE and gently simmer for about 5 minutes.

3 Take off the heat and liquidise using a blender or food processor. Pour back into the saucepan and add the herbs, crème fraîche and Parmesan, stirring well. Check for seasoning and serve with crusty bread.

Conventional Cooking:
Cook the courgettes in a frying pan over a medium heat on the hob. Pour in the stock and continue as above, over a medium heat.

roasted garlic and onion soup

serves 6

500 g medium-sized white onions (about 10)
4 whole heads of garlic, unpeeled
3 tbsp olive oil
1.5 litres beef stock
100 ml white wine

4 medium potatoes, peeled and chopped
160 g Gruyère cheese, grated, for garnish
6 slices French bread, toasted
salt and pepper

1 Cut the onions in half, leaving the outer skin on. Put them into a bowl and add the garlic heads. Pour in about 3 tablespoons of olive oil and toss them together, making sure they are well coated in the oil.

2 Tip the mixture into the large Aga roasting tin and slide the tin onto the floor of the ROASTING OVEN and cook for 20 minutes. Stir the onions and garlic in the tin and move the tin to the second set of runners and cook for a further 20-25 minutes or until they are soft and caramelised.

3 Remove the onions and garlic from their skins and put them into a deep saucepan. Pour in the stock, white wine and potatoes. Bring to the boil on the BOILING PLATE, then transfer to the SIMMERING OVEN for 35 minutes or until the potatoes are soft. Whiz the soup in a food processor or with hand-held blender and taste for seasoning – the amount of salt and pepper you add depends how your stock is seasoned.

4 Ladle into soup bowls and top each one with a toasted slice of baguette and some Gruyère cheese sprinkled over the top.

Conventional Cooking:
Pre-heat the oven to 220°C/425°F/gas 7 and roast the garlic for about an hour. Cook the soup on the hob over a medium heat.

rillettes of duck with toasted brioche

serves 4-6

1 duck, weighing about 2.75 kg
150 g duck fat, cut from the duck
350 g pork fat
125 g pork fillet, cut into large pieces
1 garlic clove
1 carrot, peeled and cut in half

1 onion, peeled and cut in half
bouquet garni, made of juniper berries, thyme and sage
300 ml white wine
1 tbsp pink peppercorns, drained and rinsed
clarified butter (see page 27)
salt and pepper

1 Cut the breasts and thigh meat off the duck and save the carcass for making stock at a later date. Cut as much fat as possible off the duck meat, discarding the skin but cutting the fat into small pieces. Put the duck fat and pork fat into a casserole with 3 tablespoons of water.

2 Put the casserole on the SIMMERING PLATE and bring to a simmer. Transfer it to the SIMMERING OVEN and leave for 30-35 minutes or until all the water has evaporated and the fat has melted.

3 Add the duck meat, pork fillet, garlic, carrot, onion, salt, pepper and bouquet garni. Pour over the white wine and bring to the boil on the BOILING PLATE. Cover the casserole with a lid and transfer to the floor of the SIMMERING OVEN for 4 hours.

4 Take the casserole out of the oven and remove the vegetables and bouquet garni. Add the pink peppercorns and cover the casserole with a damp tea towel. Leave to cool in a cool, well-ventilated area.

5 When it is cool enough to handle, shred the meat with your hands and knead it so that the fat and meat is really well mixed. Spoon the rillettes into individual ramekins and cover them with a layer of clarified butter. It is best if you make these 2-3 days in advance. They will keep in the fridge for up to 5 days. Bring the rillettes back to room temperature before eating, and serve with toasted brioche.

Conventional Cooking:
Cook the duck in a casserole over a medium heat on the hob until the water has evaporated and the fat has melted. Pre-heat the oven to 120°C/250°F/gas ½ and cook for 3-4 hours.

leeks vinaigrette

serves 4

16 baby leeks (4 per person)
1 tbsp toasted pinenuts
1 tsp pink peppercorns, drained and rinsed

FOR THE DRESSING:
1 tbsp red wine vinegar
1 tbsp walnut oil
2 tbsp sunflower oil
1 tsp Dijon mustard
½ tsp sugar
salt and pepper

1 First, make the dressing by whisking the vinegar, oils, mustard, sugar, salt and pepper together.

2 Next, steam the leeks. Put the leeks into an ovenproof dish and add 3 tablespoons of water. Season with salt and pepper and cover with foil. Put the dish on the third set of runners of the ROASTING OVEN for about 10-12 minutes or until tender.

3 When they are ready, either divide the portions between each plate or pile the leeks onto one large serving platter and drizzle over the dressing, making sure the leeks are all well coated, then sprinkle over the pinenuts and peppercorns. Serve with crusty bread.

Conventional Cooking:
Pre-heat the oven to 200°C/400°F/gas 6 and bake the leeks for 15-20 minutes.

tuna pâté with ciabatta crostini and capers

serves 6

175 g unsalted butter
4 shallots, peeled and finely sliced
3 anchovy fillets
500 g tuna steaks
juice of 2 lemons
zest of 1 lemon

twist of black pepper
1 tbsp flat leaf parsley

TO SERVE:
12 ciabatta slices
1 clove garlic, peeled
large, good-quality capers

1 Gently heat 15 g of the butter in a frying pan on the SIMMERING PLATE and cook the shallots and anchovy fillets until they are soft but not coloured. Remove them from the pan and set aside.

2 Heat another 15-30 g of the butter in the same pan and cook the tuna steaks for about 3-4 minutes on each side. Remove them from the pan and let them cool to room temperature.

3 When the shallots and tuna are cool, put them and the rest of the ingredients into a food processor and whiz until very smooth. Taste for seasoning. Place the pâté into a bowl and chill in the refrigerator.

4 When you are ready to serve, toast the ciabatta bread and then rub each half with the clove of garlic. Spoon on some of the pâté and garnish with capers. Serve 2 or 3 slices per person.

Conventional Cooking:
The tuna can be cooked in a frying pan on the hob over a medium heat.

roasted root vegetable salad with garlic rouille

serves 6

4 large Desirée potatoes, peeled and cut into wedges

4 parsnips, peeled and cut in half lengthways
(or quarters if they are large)

2 bulbs of fennel, trimmed and cut into wedges

4 baby carrots

1 tbsp fresh thyme leaves

olive oil

salt and pepper

1 Put the potato wedges into a bowl of cold water for 10 minutes. Drain them well and pat dry with kitchen paper.

2 Put the potato wedges, parsnips, fennel, carrots, thyme and salt and pepper into a bowl and pour over about 2 tbsp of olive oil. Toss the vegetables so they are well coated and tip them into an Aga roasting tin.

3 Hang the tin on the second set of runners of the ROASTING OVEN and roast for 40-45 minutes until they are charred around the edges and tender. Check after 25 minutes – if the carrots and fennel are cooked, remove them and set aside until the other vegetables are done.

4 When they have finished cooking, remove the vegetables from the tin with a slotted spoon and leave them to cool to room temperature. Arrange the vegetables on plates and serve with individual bowls of rouille (see below) and crusty bread.

Conventional Cooking:
Pre-heat the oven to 220°C/425°F/gas 7 and roast for 40-45 minutes.

rouille

300 g potatoes, peeled and chopped into large chunks

2 garlic cloves, crushed

3 hard-boiled eggs, peeled and roughly chopped

300 ml olive oil

pinch of saffron

salt

freshly ground white pepper

1 Put the potatoes into a saucepan and cover with water. Bring them to the boil on the BOILING PLATE and boil for 5 minutes. Drain off all the water, put a lid on the pan and move the pan to the SIMMERING OVEN for 20-25 minutes or until the potatoes are tender.

2 When they are cooked, remove the lid and put the pan into the ROASTING OVEN for 1 minute to dry the potatoes out slightly.

3 Put a sieve over a large bowl and first rub the potatoes through the sieve, then the hard-boiled eggs. Stir them together until well mixed, then pour in the olive oil a little at a time, stirring constantly to emulsify. Season to taste with saffron, salt and white pepper.

Conventional Cooking:
Boil the potatoes for 25 minutes over a medium-high heat on the hob. Drain and leave for 5 minutes, then continue as above.

right: roasted root vegetable salad with garlic rouille

arbroath smokies with pernod and crème fraîche

serves 6

30 g butter
1 small onion, peeled and chopped finely
8 Arbroath smokies, skinned, boned and flaked
2 tbsp Pernod

3 tbsp crème fraîche
feathery fronds of a fennel bulb, chopped
salt and pepper

1 Put the butter and onion into a large frying pan and cook them on the floor of the ROASTING OVEN for 10 minutes or until they are soft but not coloured.

2 Transfer the frying pan to the SIMMERING PLATE and add the smokies and Pernod. Cook for a few minutes then add the crème fraîche and cook for 2 more minutes.

3 Sprinkle in the fennel tops, stir and spoon into six individual shallow warmed dishes. Serve with buttered rye bread.

Conventional Cooking:

Cook in a large frying pan on the hob over a medium heat.

flat bread with parma ham and taleggio

serves 6

12 large tortilla breads
olive oil
12 slices Parma ham
1 large bunch of basil leaves
240 g Taleggio cheese, sliced thinly
bag of rocket salad

FOR THE BALSAMIC DRESSING:
1 tbsp aged balsamic vinegar
1 tbsp extra virgin olive oil
2 tbsp olive oil
salt and pepper

1 Take six tortillas and lay them out on a flat surface. Drizzle a small amount of olive oil over each tortilla and lay two slices of ham on the bottom. Divide the basil between them and top each with the sliced Taleggio. Cover with the remaining tortillas and gently press together.

2 Lift the lid of the SIMMERING PLATE and place a round piece of Bake-O-Glide on the hot surface. Wipe with a little olive oil and lay the filled flat bread directly on the hot surface. Cook for about 3-4 minutes on each side or until they are golden and the cheese has melted. Repeat for each flat bread, keeping the cooked ones warm on a warmed plate covered with a clean tea towel.

3 Whisk all the dressing ingredients together.

4 Cut the tortillas into quarters with a pair of scissors and divide the slices between 6 plates. Sprinkle them with salt and black pepper and serve with a rocket salad dressed with balsamic dressing.

Conventional Cooking:

Heat a frying pan over a medium heat. Wipe the merest hint of oil over the frying pan and cook the tortillas in the pan for 3-4 minutes on each side and serve as above.

oven-baked avocados

serves 2

2 large ripe avocados
2 spring onions, trimmed and sliced
1 tbsp tomato purée
pinch of flaked chillies
1 tbsp fresh basil, shredded
1 clove garlic, peeled and crushed

100 g sun-blushed tomatoes
50 g black olives, stones removed
1 ball mozzarella, sliced thinly
1 tbsp olive oil
salt and pepper
focaccia bread, to serve

1 Cut the avocados in half, remove the stone and skin, and place in an ovenproof dish and set aside.

2 In a bowl mix the spring onions, tomato purée, flaked chilli, basil, garlic, sun-blushed tomatoes and olives together and check the seasoning.

3 Place the avocados on a baking sheet. Spoon the mixture into the avocados, cover with the sliced mozzarella and drizzle over the olive oil. Bake on the third set of runners in the ROASTING OVEN for 10-15 minutes or until the cheese is melted and golden.

Conventional Cooking:
Pre-heat the oven to 220°C/425°F/gas 7 and bake the avocados for 15-20 minutes.

asparagus and mint mini frittatas

serves 6

olive oil
9 large eggs
250 g asparagus, blanched and cut into tips and 2 cm pieces

100 g freshly grated Parmesan cheese
1 heaped tbsp fresh mint, shredded
salt and pepper

1 Brush the insides of a muffin tin with olive oil.

2 Break the eggs into a large bowl and beat lightly. Stir in the rest of the ingredients and pour the egg mixture into the muffin tin. Place the tin on the third set of runners in the ROASTING OVEN and cook for 10-15 minutes or until the frittatas are puffy and golden.

3 Serve the frittatas straight away or at room temperature, garnished with more Parmesan. Serve with a green salad and cherry tomatoes. These are also great to pack up for a picnic.

Conventional Cooking:
Pre-heat the oven to 200°C/400°F/gas 6 and continue as above.

grilled tiger prawn and fennel salad

The prawns can be prepared several hours in advance, assembling the dish at the last minute, making this a perfect summer dinner party starter.

serves 6

1 kg raw tiger prawns, shelled and deveined

1 yellow pepper, roasted, skinned, de-seeded and cut into chunks

1 red pepper, roasted, skinned, de-seeded and cut into chunks

1 large head fennel, trimmed and sliced very thinly

1 head radicchio, torn into medium pieces

1 bag wild rocket

1 heaped tbsp chopped flat-leaf parsley

FOR THE DRESSING:

juice of 1 lemon

3 tbsp light olive oil

Maldon salt, to taste

pepper

1 In a bowl, whisk the ingredients for the dressing together until well combined, then set aside.

2 Heat a ridged grill pan in the ROASTING OVEN. Put the tiger prawns into a bowl, add 2 tablespoons of the dressing and toss well to coat.

3 Take grill pan out of the ROASTING OVEN and put onto the BOILING PLATE. Cook the prawns in batches (do not overcrowd the pan) for about 2 minutes on each side. If the heat is too intense, transfer the pan to the SIMMERING PLATE. Don't overcook them or they will be tough.

4 Put the cooked prawns into a bowl and add the peppers and fennel. Deglaze the grill pan with some of the dressing and pour over the prawns. Pour over the remaining dressing and leave to cool.

5 When you are ready to serve, arrange the radicchio and rocket on a large platter and put the tiger prawn and pepper salad on top. Garnish with flat-leaf parsley and serve with lots of crusty bread.

Conventional Cooking:

Pre-heat a grill pan over a high heat until smoking and cook prawns as above. Turn the heat down if it becomes too hot.

family food

family food – monday to friday cooking

In my Aga demonstrations over the years, I have noticed that the recipes that everyone wants are the ones which you can go home and make that night for dinner. Cooking for a family day in, day out can become a drag, so here are some recipes to alleviate the boredom of what to have for dinner. It is often the decision of what to cook rather than the actual cooking part that is the most tedious!

pasta

Pasta is that good old family standby, and it can be cooked very easily on the BOILING PLATE or SIMMERING PLATE. Bring a large pot of water to the boil, generously add salt, then when the water reaches a rolling boil, add the pasta and cook for however many minutes the instructions say on the package.

alsatian potato torte

serves 4-6

15 g unsalted butter, cut into cubes, plus a little more for greasing the dish

750 g waxy potatoes, peeled

2 fat cloves garlic, peeled and thinly sliced

2 tsp caraway seeds or cumin

250 g Munster cheese, sliced

175 ml double cream

500 g pack puff pastry

1 egg yolk

salt and pepper

1 Grease an ovenproof dish with some of the butter.

2 Cook the potatoes in a saucepan of boiling water on the BOILING PLATE for about 8 minutes. Drain and slice.

3 Build up layers in the prepared dish in the following order: potatoes, garlic, salt, pepper, caraway or cumin seeds, Munster cheese, cream. Repeat until all the ingredients are used up.

4 Roll out the pastry and top the potatoes with it, tucking in the pastry. Brush the top with a beaten egg yolk. Slide a grid shelf onto the fourth set of runners in the ROASTING OVEN and place the dish on the shelf. Cook for 45-50 minutes or until the pastry is puffed up and golden. Slide the COLD PLAIN SHELF onto the second set of runners 20 minutes into the cooking time.

5 Cut the torte into slices and serve warm with a green salad with French dressing.

Conventional Cooking:
Pre-heat the oven to 200°C/400°F/gas 6 and bake in the middle of the oven for 40-45 minutes.

free-form roasted vegetable pie

Don't be alarmed if the pastry of this rustic-style pie crumbles and some patching up is required. Whatever you do, try not to over-work the dough.

serves 4 generously

FOR THE PIE CRUST:	FOR THE ROASTED VEGETABLES:
340 g plain flour	**2 red onions, peeled and cut into segments**
225 g cold butter	**2 garlic cloves, whole not peeled**
80 g Parmesan cheese, grated	**2 red peppers, deseeded and sliced into large pieces**
1 large egg	**2 yellow peppers, deseeded and sliced into large pieces**
1 tbsp water	**1 small tin of anchovy fillets in olive oil, drained with the oil reserved**
salt and pepper	**2 tbsp mixed fresh herbs (such as flat-leaf parsley, tarragon and thyme)**
	50 g black olives, pitted
	1 egg yolk, beaten
	30 g Parmesan cheese, grated

1 Make the pastry in a food processor or by hand. Process the flour with the butter until the mixture resembles coarse breadcrumbs. Add the cheese and egg, then season. Process with the water until the dough just comes together. Tip it out onto a floured surface and knead lightly until smooth. Wrap in a plastic bag and rest in the refrigerator for 1 hour.

2 Put the onions, garlic cloves and peppers into a bowl and pour over the reserved oil from the anchovy fillets. Season with salt and pepper and toss it all together to coat everything well. (If you need a bit more oil, pour in some olive oil.)

3 Spread the vegetables out onto a shallow Aga baking tray and hang it on the first set of runners in the ROASTING OVEN for 20 minutes, then move it to the floor of the oven for a further 20 minutes or until the vegetables are soft and charred around the edges. Set aside to cool. This can be done 24 hours in advance.

4 When you are ready to assemble the pie, roll out the pastry on a lightly floured surface to a thickness of 5 mm. Carefully transfer the pastry to a 25-cm pie dish and let the excess dough hang over the sides. Spoon in the roasted vegetables and herbs. Squeeze out the garlic from their papery cases over the peppers, then scatter over the olives and anchovies. Fold in the sides of the pastry dough, leaving the centre of the pie exposed. Brush with a little beaten egg and sprinkle over the grated Parmesan cheese.

5 Bake for 20 minutes on the floor of the ROASTING OVEN, then move it to the fourth set of runners for a further 15 minutes. If the pastry browns too quickly, slide the COLD PLAIN SHELF onto the third set of runners.

Conventional Cooking:
Pre-heat the oven to 200°C/400°F/gas 6 and bake in the middle of the oven for 35-40 minutes.

devilled herring roes on toast

serves 4

1 tbsp flour	1 tbsp flat-leaf parsley, chopped
2 x 100 g tins herring roes, drained	dash of Tabasco
80 g butter	80 ml double cream
4 slices buttered toast	salt and pepper
1 tsp Dijon mustard	

1 Season the flour with the salt and pepper and coat the herring roes in the seasoned flour.

2 Heat the butter in a frying pan on the SIMMERING PLATE and fry the herring roes for 3-4 minutes. Remove them with a slotted spoon and divide them between the slices of toast. Keep warm.

3 Add the mustard, parsley, Tabasco and cream to the pan and scrape up all the bits from the bottom. Check the seasoning. Let it bubble for a minute, then pour over the herring roes and serve.

Conventional Cooking:
Cook in a frying pan as above, over a medium heat on the hob.

old-fashioned meatloaf

serves 6

FOR THE MEATLOAF:	4 tbsp fresh breadcrumbs, from a day-old country loaf
250 g minced pork	1 tbsp flat leaf parsley, chopped
250 g minced beef	salt and pepper
250 g minced veal	
2 large eggs	FOR THE TOPPING:
100 ml tomato ketchup	3 tbsp tomato ketchup
2 tbsp Worcestershire sauce	2½ tsp mustard powder
2 level tsp mustard powder	2 tbsp brown sugar
1 large onion, peeled and very finely chopped	6-8 rashers pancetta or smoked streaky bacon

1 In a large bowl mix all the meatloaf ingredients, using your hands to knead until thoroughly combined. Shape the meat mixture into a long loaf so that it will fit into the half-size Aga roasting tin. The mix should be wet enough to hold together.

2 Put the half-size Aga grill rack into the half-size Aga roasting tin and place the meatloaf on it.

3 To make the topping, mix together the ketchup, mustard powder and sugar. Brush it onto the meatloaf and arrange the pancetta slices over it.

4 Cook the meatloaf on the fourth set of runners in the ROASTING OVEN for 45-60 minutes. If the top is browning too quickly, slide the COLD PLAIN SHELF in on the second set of runners after about 30 minutes or so. Serve in slices with plenty of mashed potatoes, peas and tomato ketchup.

Conventional Cooking:
Pre-heat the oven to 200°C/400°F/gas 6 and bake for 1-1½ hours.

bacon and egg pie

serves 6

300 g bacon, cut into cubes or large strips
6 hard-boiled eggs, cut in half
80 g Cheddar cheese, grated
1 egg, beaten
salt and pepper

FOR THE SAVOURY DOUGH:
340 g plain flour
225 g butter, softened
1 large egg

FOR THE CHEESE SAUCE:
15 g butter
15 g plain flour
300 ml milk, warmed
50 g mature Cheddar cheese, grated
pinch of powdered mustard

1 Make the pastry in a food processor or by hand. Process the flour with the butter until the mixture resembles coarse breadcrumbs. Add the egg and season. Process until the dough just comes together. Tip it out onto a floured surface and knead lightly until smooth. Wrap in a plastic bag and rest in the refrigerator for 1 hour.

2 Make the cheese sauce. Melt the butter in a saucepan on the SIMMERING PLATE. Stirring constantly with a wooden spoon, add the flour. Cook for 2 minutes. Do not allow the mix to brown. Gradually add the milk little by little, stirring constantly to prevent lumps forming. Continue to cook until the sauce comes to the boil and thickens. Add the cheese and mustard. Stir until it has melted and check for seasoning. Simmer for 2-3 minutes. Set aside to cool.

3 Fry the bacon in a pan on the SIMMERING PLATE until it is crispy around the edges. Drain on kitchen paper.

4 Divide the pastry in half. Roll it out so you have a piece to line a 20-cm pie dish and a piece to cover the pie.

5 Put the boiled egg halves, cut side down, and the bacon into the bottom of the pie dish. Pour over the cheese sauce and scatter over the grated cheese. Roll on the pastry lid, making a slit in the middle. Brush the top with the beaten egg.

6 Put the grid shelf on the fourth set of runners in the ROASTING OVEN and cook the pie for 20-30 minutes. Slide the COLD PLAIN SHELF onto the second set of runners if the top is browning too fast. Then transfer to the floor of the ROASTING OVEN for 5 minutes. Remove the pie from the oven and let it cool. For 4-oven Aga owners, use the BAKING OVEN as above, then transfer the pie to the ROASTING OVEN floor for the final 5-10 minutes. Serve at room temperature with a green salad.

Conventional Cooking:
Pre-heat the oven to 190°C/375°F/gas 5 and bake in the middle of the oven for 35-40 minutes.

baked eggs in beefsteak tomatoes with herbs

per person:

1 large firm, slightly under-ripe beefsteak tomato	**1 tbsp double cream**
1 tbsp melted butter	**1 tsp finely chopped fresh tarragon**
1 medium-sized egg	**salt and pepper**

1 Cut the top of the tomato off about one-quarter of the way down from the stem end and carefully scoop out the seeds. Try not to break or split the tomato. Brush the inside of the tomato with the melted butter and season with a little salt and pepper.

2 Break the egg into the buttered tomato, season with salt and pepper. Pour over the double cream, sprinkle in the tarragon and set the tomato on a baking tray.

3 Slide the tray onto the third set of runners in the ROASTING OVEN and cook for 5-8 minutes or until the egg is cooked. (The key thing to watch out for is if the tomato is too ripe, it may split during baking.)

4 Remove from the oven and place the baked tomato on a dish with a few chicory leaves. Garnish with some more fresh tarragon leaves if desired and serve with warm bread.

Conventional Cooking:

Pre-heat the oven to 200°C/400°F/gas 6 and bake for about 8-10 minutes.

savoury egg meringue

Another delicious way to serve this is to add a slice of ham or smoked salmon beneath the meringue or substitute the cheese with chopped chives.

per person:

1 slice of brioche or other similar bread	**30 g mature Cheddar cheese, finely grated**
butter	**salt and pepper**
1 large egg, separated	

1 Toast the brioche using the Aga toaster and spread with butter. Put the toast on a shallow Aga baking tray. Make a dent in the centre of the toast and carefully slide the yolk into it.

2 In a very clean bowl, beat the egg white until stiff. Fold in the cheese and season with salt and pepper. Carefully spoon the egg white over the egg yolk and the top of the toast completely so all you can see is a fluffy white mass.

3 Slide the baking tray onto the third set of runners of the ROASTING OVEN and cook for about 5-7 minutes or until the meringue is starting to brown and rising a little. Serve straight away.

Conventional Cooking:

Pre-heat the oven to 220°C/425°F/gas 7 and cook for 7-8 minutes.

right: baked eggs in beefsteak tomatoes with herbs

braised lamb with prunes and apricots

This is a great dish because you can put it in first thing in the morning and forget about it.

serves 6-8

3 tbsp olive oil	350 ml vegetable or chicken stock
2 kg trimmed lamb neck fillets, cut into 2 cm chunks	120 g chopped dried apricots
2 large onions, peeled and cut into segments	120 g chopped dried prunes
2 tbsp flour	salt and pepper
100 ml red wine	

1 In a large casserole on the SIMMERING PLATE, heat 2 tablespoons of oil until it is smoking and brown the lamb in batches, until it is all lightly coloured. Tip the meat onto a plate and set aside. (If you wish, you can brown meat in a shallow baking tray at the top of the ROASTING OVEN and then move the tray without turning the meat to the ROASTING OVEN floor.)

2 Add the remaining oil to the casserole and fry the onions until charred around the edges. Sprinkle in the flour and make sure it coats all of the onion mix and soaks up all the fat. Pour in the wine and then the stock a little at a time, whisking until it is all in and there are no lumps.

3 Add the apricots, prunes, salt and pepper and lamb and bring to the boil. Cover with a lid and transfer to the floor of the SIMMERING OVEN. Cook for 2½-3 hours minimum or leave it in the Aga until you get home.

Conventional Cooking:
Pre-heat the oven to 140°C/275°F/gas 1 and cook for 2½-3½ hours.

turkey burgers with tomato confit

You can make the tomato confit in advance and store it in the fridge for up to one week. It is delicious with so many things; serve it warm or at room temperature.

serves 4

FOR THE BURGERS:
900 g minced turkey
½ tbsp fresh thyme leaves
3 spring onions, white part only, very finely chopped
1 tbsp Worcestershire sauce
1 tbsp tomato purée
salt and pepper

FOR THE TOMATO CONFIT:
1 kg ripe vine tomatoes, cut in half
6 garlic cloves, peeled and sliced thinly
100 g fresh sourdough breadcrumbs
1 tbsp fresh flat-leaf parsley, chopped
3 tbsp olive oil
4 soft round wholewheat burger buns, to serve
mayonnaise, to serve
curly endive, to garnish

1 In a large bowl mix all the burger ingredients together by hand, making sure they are all well combined. Shape the meat into four round patties, place on a piece of greaseproof paper and refrigerate for an hour.

2 To make the confit, put the tomatoes, cut side up, in an Aga roasting tin. Scatter the garlic slices over them and season with salt and pepper. Mix together the breadcrumbs and parsley and cover the tomatoes with them. Drizzle over the olive oil. Slide the tin onto the second set of runners in the ROASTING OVEN and bake for 45-60 minutes or until soft and sizzling. Transfer to a bowl and set aside.

3 To cook the burgers, heat a frying pan or Aga grill pan on the floor of the ROASTING OVEN until it is very hot and smoking. Put the burgers into it and put the pan back onto the ROASTING OVEN floor and cook for 8 minutes on each side.

4 Toast the burger buns using the Aga toaster; spread a little mayonnaise on the bottom half of the bun and a little of the curly endive. Put the turkey burger on top and spoon on some of the tomato confit. Serve with coleslaw.

Conventional cooking:.

To cook the confit, pre-heat the oven to 200°C/400°F/ gas 6 and cook as above. To cook the burgers, pre-heat a grill pan and cook the burgers under a medium heat.

stir-fried chicken with soba noodles

serves 4

40 ml groundnut oil	50 ml soy sauce
1 clove garlic, crushed	240 ml chicken stock
8 cm piece of fresh ginger, peeled and cut into strips	½ tsp brown sugar
2 chicken breasts, skinned and cut into thin strips	½ tbsp cornflour, mixed with 1 tbsp water to form a thin paste
10-12 shiitake mushrooms, sliced	½ tsp sesame oil
300 g broccoli, cut into spears	500 g soba noodles, cooked (or substitute cooked linguine or spaghetti)
1 small bunch spring onions, trimmed and cut into diagonal chunks	sesame seeds, to garnish
½ tbsp rice vinegar	

1 Put a large bowl into the SIMMERING OVEN to warm.

2 Heat three-quarters of the groundnut oil in a wok on the SIMMERING PLATE. Add the garlic and half the ginger. Cook gently to infuse the oil with the flavourings. When the garlic and ginger turn brown, remove them with a slotted spoon and discard.

3 Transfer the wok to the BOILING PLATE and quickly brown the chicken pieces. Add the mushrooms, broccoli, spring onions and the rest of the ginger. Cook for 3-4 minutes, stirring the chicken and vegetables constantly.

4 Add the vinegar, soy sauce, stock, sugar and cornflour paste. Bring to the boil and cook for 2 minutes or until the sauce starts to thicken. Take the bowl out of the SIMMERING OVEN; transfer the chicken and vegetables to the warmed bowl and set aside.

5 Add the rest of the groundnut oil and the sesame oil to the wok and heat the noodles through, adding a little of the sauce from the bowl of chicken. Divide the noodles between warmed serving bowls and top with the chicken and vegetables. Garnish with a sprinkling of sesame seeds.

Conventional Cooking:

Use a wok over a high heat and cook as above.

steak sandwich with oven chips

This is more than just a sandwich – it's a whole mood!

serves 4

4 x 150 g rib eye steaks, beaten out so they are thin
4 slices rye bread, toasted
4 eggs

FOR THE WELSH RAREBIT SAUCE:
50 g butter
230 g extra mature Cheddar cheese
150 ml Guinness or stout
1 tsp mustard powder
2 egg yolks, slightly beaten
½ tbsp Worcestershire sauce

1 To make the Welsh rarebit sauce, melt the butter in a saucepan on the SIMMERING PLATE; add the cheese, stir, then add the stout slowly, stirring all the time until the mix is smooth. Stirring constantly, add the mustard powder, egg yolks and Worcestershire sauce and cook until the sauce is thick and glossy. Check for seasoning. Do not let the cheese mix boil or bubble or it will become lumpy. Set aside.

2 Heat the Aga grill pan on the floor of the ROASTING OVEN until it is very hot. Remove the pan from the oven and put it on the BOILING PLATE. Lay the steaks in the pan and cook to your liking, about 1-2 minutes each side. Set aside and keep warm.

3 Line the half-size Aga baking tray with Bake-O-Glide.

Spread the Welsh rarebit mix on the toast and place on the baking tray. Slide the tray onto the first set of runners in the ROASTING OVEN for about 2 minutes or until they start to bubble.

4 While the rarebit is in the oven, fry the eggs on the SIMMERING PLATE (either grease the surface or use the pre-cut round disc of Bake-O-Glide – see page 14).

5 To assemble the sandwich, remove the rarebit from the oven, put the steak on it, then top the steak with the fried egg. Eat immediately.

Conventional Cooking:
Cook the sauce over a gentle heat on the hob. Fry the steaks and eggs in a frying pan on the hob.

aga oven chips

Adjust the quantities to suit the numbers. The method is the same.

1 Peel some potatoes and cut them into thick strips. Soak the potatoes in cold water for 10 minutes and drain very well on a tea towel. The drier they are, the better.

2 Put the potatoes into a large bowl and pour in some sunflower oil – about 1 tablespoon for every 2 potatoes. Toss the potatoes in the oil and make sure they are all evenly coated.

3 Spread the potatoes on a large baking tray and cook them on the ROASTING OVEN floor for 35-45 minutes, turning occasionally, until they are brown and crisp on all sides. Remove them from the oven, sprinkle generously with salt and serve.

Conventional Cooking:
Pre-heat the oven to 220°C/425°F/gas 7 and continue as above.

parmigiano, thyme and rosemary risotto

Simple, fresh ingredients and good stock are essential to make risotto, and there can be no quicker way to make stock than in an Aga.

serves 6

olive oil	200 g Parmigiano Reggiano cheese, grated
1 onion, peeled and finely chopped	generous knob of butter
1 clove garlic, peeled and finely chopped	½ tbsp rosemary
500 g arborio rice	½ tbsp thyme
1 glass white wine	salt and pepper
1 litre chicken stock, heated	

1 Put a tablespoon of olive oil into a heavy-bottomed frying pan and place it on the floor of the ROASTING OVEN to heat up. When it is hot, take out and add the onion and put back on the ROASTING OVEN floor for about 10 minutes to soften.

2 When the onion is ready, place pan on the SIMMERING PLATE and add salt and pepper, the garlic and rice. Stirring constantly, coat the rice in the onion and oil mixture until the rice becomes translucent.

3 Pour in the wine and stir until it is almost all evaporated, then add the stock. Stir and bring to the boil, then place the pan on the SIMMERING OVEN floor for 15-20 minutes.

4 When the liquid has nearly all been absorbed and the rice is tender but still has a bit of a bite, take the pan out of the oven and stir in the Parmigiano cheese, a knob of butter and fresh herbs. Check the seasoning and serve with a green salad.

Conventional Cooking:
Pre-heat the oven to 150°C/300°F/gas 2 and when all of the stock has been added to the rice, place the pan in the centre of the oven and cook for 30 minutes.

hot open salmon sandwich

serves 4

	FOR THE SAUCE:
4 salmon fillets, not too thick	2 tbsp Dijon mustard
grapeseed oil	3 tbsp brown sugar
4 slices rye bread	1 tsp grapeseed oil
salt and pepper	1 tbsp freshly chopped dill
1 bag washed and prepared wild rocket leaves	

1 Put an Aga grill pan on the floor of the ROASTING OVEN to heat up.

2 Meanwhile, make the sauce. Put the mustard powder, sugar, oil and 2½ tablespoons of water into a bowl and mix well. Stir in the chopped dill. Set aside.

3 Brush the salmon fillets with a little oil and season with salt and pepper. When the grill pan is smoking, put it on the BOILING PLATE and lay the salmon in the pan. Put the pan back on the floor of the ROASTING OVEN and cook for another 3-4 minutes. When the salmon is cooked, take the pan out and set aside.

4 Toast the bread in the Aga toaster and put one slice on each plate. Top each slice with rocket and put a salmon fillet on the rocket. Drizzle over some sauce and serve.

Conventional Cooking:
Heat a grill pan on top of a hob until smoking and cook as above.

grilled pork chops with honey and meaux mustard

serves 4

4 pork chops	1 tbsp honey
½ tbsp mild olive oil	1 tbsp Meaux mustard
½ onion, peeled and very finely chopped	80 ml crème fraîche
60 ml cider	salt and pepper

1 Heat the Aga grill pan on the floor of the ROASTING OVEN until it smokes. Season the pork chops with salt and pepper.

2 Take the grill pan out of the oven and put it on the BOILING PLATE. Add the chops and put the pan back on the ROASTING OVEN floor for 4-5 minutes (this depends on how thick the chops are). Turn the chops and cook for a further 4-5 minutes. When they are cooked, transfer them to a warmed plate, cover and rest.

3 While the chops are cooking you can start the sauce. Heat up the oil in a frying pan on the SIMMERING PLATE and cook the onion until soft and starting to caramelise around the edges. Add the cider and cook for 1 minute to burn off the alcohol. Stir in the honey, mustard and crème fraîche. Add any pan juices left in the grill pan and check for seasoning. Bubble the sauce up for 2 minutes and serve with the pork chops. Oven chips are great with these chops (see page 56).

Conventional Cooking:
Pre-heat a grill pan over a high heat until smoking and cook the chops as above. To cook the mustard sauce, use a frying pan set over a medium heat and continue as above.

right: hot open salmon sandwich

chicken
and game

Chicken is the 'Little Black Dress' of the kitchen! I could eat it every day and find it the most versatile meat to cook – nothing beats a good roast chicken. Naturally low in fat, game such as pheasant and woodcock is a healthy and full-flavoured option when simply cooked, and it is its seasonality that makes it so special and eagerly awaited.

roast chicken

This method is for roasting chicken and all poultry except large turkeys. Line the roasting tin with Bake-O-Glide. Cut an onion in half (use two for a large chicken) and place the chicken on top of the onion. Stuff the cavity of the chicken with herbs, onion or lemon and season with salt and pepper. Rub over butter or oil or lay strips of bacon over the chicken; rub in more salt and pepper. Slide the tin onto the lowest set of runners in the ROASTING OVEN and set the timer (see right). Check halfway through cooking and cover the chicken with foil if it is browning too quickly. To test if the chicken is cooked, pierce the thigh with a skewer; if the juices run clear, it is cooked. If they are pink or red, the chicken is not ready so cook for a little longer. Rest the chicken for 15 minutes before carving.

Approximate timings for roasting a whole chicken:
900 g chicken (small): 35-45 minutes
1.5 kg chicken (medium): 45-60 minutes
2 kg chicken (large): 1½-1¾ hours
3 kg chicken (very large): 2 hours

roast pheasant

Line the roasting tin with Bake-O-Glide. Place the bird or birds in the tin and generously rub with butter or lard (or even cover with the paper that the butter is wrapped in) and season with salt and pepper. If you wish, cover the breasts with bacon. Stuff the cavity of the pheasant with half an onion or apple and season with salt and pepper. Slide the tin onto the third set of runners of the ROASTING OVEN and set the timer for 45-50 minutes. Halfway through cooking, baste. To test if the pheasant is cooked, pierce the thigh with a skewer; if the juices run clear, it is cooked. Serve with bread sauce, game chips and fried breadcrumbs. Be careful not to overcook game. As the fat content is lower, it does have a tendency to dry out.

roast partridge, grouse, woodcock, snipe and quail

Cook as for pheasant but adjust the cooking times and accompaniments.
Partridge: Roast for 30-35 minutes and serve with quince cheese or redcurrant jelly.
Grouse: Roast for 20-30 minutes and serve on croûtes of fried bread spread with the pan-fried liver of the grouse if you are lucky enough to have it.
Woodcock, snipe and quail: Roast for 12-15 minutes. Serve woodcock and snipe on croûtes (as for grouse). Quail is such a versatile bird that it can be served in almost any way you wish. On average, allow 1½ birds per person.

roast turkey

The Aga can accommodate a turkey up to 12.5 kg and I recommend using the Aga turkey roasting tin. There are two methods of roasting turkey: the slow roasting method, which can be done overnight, and the conventional method. The advantage of the slow method is that you don't have to worry about the turkey and the Roasting Oven will be available for cooking all the traditional trimmings. Timings are approximate and very much depend of the size of the bird. The timings may have to be increased for older Agas if you use the slow roasting method.

The conventional method of cooking the turkey will use up quite a lot of heat so planning and preparation are very important.

Preparing a fresh turkey
Wash the turkey with water and pat dry with kitchen towel. Stuff only the neck end of the bird, put a couple of onions into the body cavity and season well with salt and pepper. Put the turkey into the roasting tin. Do not truss the bird. Generously brush melted clarified butter all over the bird (see page 27). Season with salt. The secret of a succulent golden bird is in the basting. Leave the pot of clarified butter at the back of the Aga so that it is in easy reach for basting about every 30 minutes if cooking the bird conventionally.

Slow roasting method
Place the roasting tin directly on the floor of the ROASTING OVEN and cook for about 1 hour or until the turkey is browned. A larger turkey may take longer to brown. It is essential to give the turkey a real blast of heat for a good amount of time for food safety. When it

is browned, baste with the clarified butter, cover loosely with foil and move to the SIMMERING OVEN for the following times:

3.6-4.5 kg: 3-6 hours
5-7.25 kg: 5-8½ hours
7.25-9 kg: 8½-11 hours
9-11 kg: 11-13½ hours
11-12.8 kg: 13½-15½ hours
All times are approximate.

Conventional or fast roasting method
Place the roasting tin on the floor of the ROASTING OVEN. After about 1 hour, or when the turkey is browned, cover loosely with foil and cook for the following times:

3.6-4.5 kg: 1¾-2 hours
5-7.25 kg: 2-2½ hours
7.25-9 kg: 2½-3 hours
9-11 kg: 3½-4½ hours
11-12.8 kg 4½-5½ hours
All times are approximate

The turkey is done when the thigh juices run clear when pierced with a skewer. Rest the turkey for at least 20 minutes. A large bird will stay hot for a long time and can withstand a long resting time. Take this into consideration when working out your cooking timetable.

When using the conventional roasting method, you can start cooking the turkey breast side down, turning it breast side up about 45 minutes before the end of the cooking time. This way of cooking the turkey ensures the breast meat will not be dry.

spatchcock poussins
with parsley and pinenut dressing

serves 6

6 butterflied spatchcock poussins (ask your butcher to prepare them)

FOR THE DRESSING:

40 g raisins

juice of ½ lemon

100 ml olive oil

2 tbsp chopped flat-leaf parsley

60 g lightly toasted pinenuts

salt and pepper

1 First make the dressing. Put the raisins into a bowl and soak them in boiling water for 5 minutes, then drain. Whisk the lemon juice and oil together in a small bowl. Add the raisins, parsley and pinenuts and season with salt and pepper. Set aside. If you make this ahead of time, leave out the pinenuts until you are ready to serve. This dressing should be served at room temperature.

2 Heat a griddle pan in the ROASTING OVEN until it is smoking. Transfer the pan to the BOILING PLATE and seal the poussins in the pan on both sides. You are aiming for charred grill marks on the birds. If the pan is too hot, transfer it to the SIMMERING PLATE.

3 When you have sealed all the birds. put them on a baking tray, season with salt, and cook in the ROASTING

OVEN for 10-15 minutes, or until they are cooked through. When they are done leave them to rest for about 10 minutes. (Any of the juices that are left in the pan or tray should be poured into the dressing.)

4 Serve the poussins with the pinenut dressing spooned over the top.

Conventional Cooking:

Heat the griddle pan on the hob and pre-heat oven to 200°C/400°F/gas 6. Seal the poussins in the griddle pan on the hob, then place them in the pre-heated oven and continue as above. Timings may vary a little so check the birds after 15 minutes – they may need a few minutes more.

pheasant sausages

serves 4

100 g butter, at the cold side of room temperature

1 kg minced pheasant meat, well chilled

200 g shallots, peeled and finely diced

1 tsp thyme leaves

75 g vacuum-packed chestnuts, chopped

salt and pepper

1 Beat the butter into the pheasant meat and the other ingredients in a large bowl. Do this as quickly as possible as you want to keep the whole thing as cold as possible.

2 Lay out two 40 cm pieces of cling film on a work surface. Pile about 2 tablespoons of the meat onto the cling film and shape into a sausage shape. Roll up the sausage in the cling film, tightly twisting the ends together so that the sausage is tightly bound. Repeat until all of the mix is used. Chill the sausages for 3-4 hours.

3 To cook, bring a large pan of water to the boil on the BOILING PLATE, then drop the cling film-wrapped sausages into the water and cook at a simmer for 3-5 minutes or until the sausages are cooked. Remove the cling film and serve with braised red cabbage and mashed potatoes.

Conventional Cooking:

Boil the water on the hob and proceed as above.

chicken roasted on freshly baked focaccia bread

We have a brilliant team at The George Hotel. Our chef, Kevin Mangeolles, is a constant inspiration and his passion and knowledge about food is enviable. This is a dish he devised for one of my demonstrations as he thought it would be a perfect Aga recipe and, as usual, he was right!

serves 2 generously

1 quantity of focaccia bread dough (see page 151)

olive oil

1 kg free-range chicken, trimmed (ask your butcher to prepare it for you)

1 tbsp rosemary sprigs

2 cloves garlic, peeled and sliced

6 cherry tomatoes

1 Roll the bread dough into a long sausage shape, set aside. Line a frying pan large enough to hold the chicken and bread with greaseproof paper and set aside.

2 Heat some olive oil in another pan on the BOILING PLATE until smoking. Season the chicken with salt and seal the chicken in the hot pan. Place the sealed chicken in the prepared frying pan and wrap the dough around it so it looks like a life-saving ring. Drizzle over some more olive oil and scatter the rosemary, salt and garlic over the chicken and the dough.

3 Bake for 40 minutes on the fourth set of runners in the ROASTING OVEN. After the 40 minutes, take the chicken out and scatter over the cherry tomatoes. Cook for a further 10 minutes, test to see if the chicken is done, then remove chicken from the oven, rest for 10 minutes and serve with a green salad.

Conventional Cooking:

This chicken dish cannot be cooked successfully in a conventional oven.

pheasant with cider

serves 6 generously

2 large pheasants jointed

olive oil

2 red onions, peeled and roughly chopped

1 tbsp flour

8 juniper berries, crushed

¼ tsp ground cinnamon

¼ tsp ground cloves

¼ tsp ground coriander

2 oranges, sliced

1.5 litres dry cider

1 tbsp crème fraîche

salt and pepper

1 In a large casserole, brown the pheasant joints in the olive oil, 4 at a time, and remove them to a plate. You can do this on the BOILING PLATE or the floor of the ROASTING OVEN.

2 Put the onions into the casserole and cook on the SIMMERING PLATE until lightly browned, then stir in the flour and cook for 2 minutes. Add the juniper berries, spices, salt and pepper and the pheasant joints, layering the orange slices in between. Finally add the cider and

bring to the boil, reduce to a simmer and then simmer for 2 hours in the SIMMERING OVEN.

3 When you are ready to serve, swirl the crème fraîche into the casserole and serve with large croûtons on the side.

Conventional Cooking:

Pre-heat the oven to 150°C/300°F/gas 2 and cook for 2¾-3¾ hours.

thai green chicken

serves 6

6 chicken breasts or 12 thighs, skinned	2 tsp ground cumin
2 tbsp grapeseed oil	4 cm piece of ginger, grated
2 shallots, peeled and finely chopped	3 red chillies, deseeded and thinly sliced
2-3 lemongrass stalks, finely sliced	2 tsp fish sauce
2 cloves garlic, crushed	1 tbsp torn basil
6 spring onions	1 tbsp chopped coriander
juice and zest of 2 limes	1 tsp peanut butter
2 shredded kaffir lime leaves	400 ml coconut milk
2 tsp coriander seeds, roasted and ground	1 tbsp chopped cashew nuts, for garnish

1 Put the chicken into a large bowl and set aside.

2 Heat up a large wok on the BOILING PLATE and add the oil. Next quickly fry, in this order, the shallots, lemongrass and garlic. Add everything else except for the coconut milk, chicken and cashew nuts. Take the spices and herbs off the heat, then pour in the coconut milk. Let the sauce cool.

3 Pour the sauce over the chicken, cover with cling film and marinate in the fridge for a minimum of 2 hours – the longer the better.

4 When you are ready to cook the chicken, transfer it to a large ovenproof dish with the marinade and slide it onto the third set of runners in the ROASTING OVEN for 25 minutes. Stir it, then cover with foil and cook for another 25 minutes. The coconut milk will probably split but it won't affect the taste. Garnish the chicken with more fresh herbs and the chopped cashew nuts, and serve with jasmine rice.

Conventional Cooking:

Pre-heat the oven to 200°C/400°F/gas 6 and cook as above.

chicken in marsala wine with oranges and shallots

serves 4-6

1 tsp cardamom seeds, removed from their outer pod

1 tsp coriander seeds

30 g flour

8 chicken pieces (either a whole jointed chicken or breasts cut in half)

2 tbsp olive oil

150 g pancetta, cubed

16 shallots, peeled

300 ml marsala wine

300 ml orange juice

1 tbsp sherry vinegar

1 stick cinnamon

6 cloves garlic, peeled

1 orange, cut into thick slices

1 heaped tbsp crème fraîche

salt and pepper

1 First dry fry the cardamom and coriander seeds in a frying pan on the SIMMERING PLATE, then crush in a pestle and mortar.

2 Season the flour with salt, pepper and the spices. Mix together well. Coat each piece of chicken with the flour and set aside.

3 In a shallow casserole dish on the SIMMERING PLATE or floor of the ROASTING OVEN, heat the olive oil and cook the pancetta, then add the chicken and shallots and cook until they are all a nutty brown colour. Add any of the leftover flour and then pour in the marsala wine, orange juice, vinegar, cinnamon stick, garlic and orange slices.

4 Stir and bring to the boil on the BOILING PLATE, then transfer to the SIMMERING OVEN for 1½-2 hours, uncovered. It is ready when the juices run clear from the chicken. Stir in the crème fraîche and serve with wild rice and a green salad.

Conventional Cooking:
Pre-heat the oven to 150°C/300°F/gas 2 and cook for 2-2½ hours as above.

casseroled chicken legs with tarragon and crème fraîche

serves 4

30 g flour	100 ml chicken stock
4 chicken legs, skinned	50 ml white wine
1 tbsp sunflower oil	4 tbsp Dijon mustard
knob of butter	1 heaped tbsp tarragon leaves, roughly chopped
1 shallot, peeled and finely chopped	140 ml crème fraîche
1 clove garlic, crushed	salt and pepper
2 flat field mushrooms, finely chopped	

1 Season the flour with the salt and pepper, then coat each chicken leg in it.

2 Heat a frying pan on the floor of the ROASTING OVEN and melt the sunflower oil and butter. Brown the chicken legs in the oil and butter on the ROASTING OVEN floor and set aside. Do not discard the oil.

3 Fry the shallot, garlic and mushrooms in the frying pan on the SIMMERING PLATE until they are soft. Add any leftover flour and stir in the stock and wine. Bring to the boil and stir in the mustard and the tarragon leaves. Remove from the heat.

4 Arrange the chicken legs in a lidded casserole and pour the mustard sauce over the top, cover and cook on the third set of runners in the ROASTING OVEN for 30 minutes, then transfer the casserole to the SIMMERING OVEN for 2-2½ hours or until the chicken is cooked and tender.

5 Remove the chicken legs to a warmed plate and reduce the sauce on the SIMMERING PLATE until it has thickened a little. Whisk in the crème fraîche and check the seasoning. Serve with rice and garnish with some more tarragon leaves.

Conventional Cooking:

Pre-heat the oven to 150°C/300°F/gas 2 and cook for 2 hours as above.

herb roasted chicken with quince jelly, thyme and rosemary sauce

serves 4

2 red onions, peeled and halved

50 g butter, softened

1 tbsp fresh thyme, chopped

1 tbsp fresh rosemary, chopped

1 clove garlic, crushed

juice and zest of 1 unwaxed lemon

1 large chicken, free range if possible

salt and pepper

FOR THE SAUCE:

2 tbsp quince jelly

2 tbsp mature red wine vinegar or balsamic vinegar

2 tbsp freshly chopped thyme

2 tbsp freshly chopped rosemary

salt and pepper

1 Put the halved onions into a roasting tin, cut side down, and set aside.

2 Put the softened butter into a bowl and add the herbs, garlic, lemon juice and zest, salt and pepper, then mash with a fork to combine.

3 Gently ease off the skin of the chicken breast with your fingers, taking care not to tear the skin. Lift the loosened skin and spread the herb butter mix underneath. Place the chicken on the onions and cook on the third set of runners in the ROASTING OVEN for 1 hour or until the leg juices run clear. Cover with foil if top is browning too much. When the chicken is cooked, let it rest for 10-15 minutes before serving with the red onions and sauce.

4 To make the sauce, whisk the quince jelly, vinegar and 1-2 tablespoons water in a saucepan on the SIMMERING PLATE until melted and simmer for about 2 minutes. Take off the heat and add the herbs and salt and pepper. Check the seasoning, pour into a jug and set aside until you are ready to serve the chicken. (If the sauce is too thick, thin down with a little water.)

Conventional Cooking:

Pre-heat the oven to 200°C/400°F/gas 6 and cook the chicken for 1½-1¾ hours or until the juices run clear. Cook the sauce in a saucepan over a gentle heat on the hob.

roast partridge with foie gras and oven-dried figs

serves 6

6 large ripe figs, cut into quarters	100 ml Madeira
icing sugar, for dusting	600 ml home-made game stock
12 shallots	1 tbsp butter
6 oven-ready partridges	345 g foie gras, cubed into 2 cm pieces
clarified butter, about ½ a teacup full (see page 27)	salt and pepper

1 First make the oven-dried figs. Spread out the fig quarters on a baking tray and dust lightly with the icing sugar. Place them on the third set of runners in the SIMMERING OVEN and bake for about 30 minutes, or until dried but still supple. This can be done in advance and kept in an airtight container.

2 Cut the shallots in half and place them cut side down in a roasting tin. Season the inside of the birds with salt and put the partridges on top of the shallots. Brush over a little clarified butter and season the birds with salt and pepper. Cook on the third set of runners in the ROASTING OVEN for 20-25 minutes.

3 When they are cooked, take the tin out of the oven and remove the partridges (but not the shallots) to a warmed platter, cover with foil and let the birds rest for 15 minutes before serving.

4 While they are resting (which is imperative), finish the sauce. Take the roasting tin and deglaze with the Madeira. Add the game stock, bring to the boil and reduce until it has halved in volume. Remove the shallots with a slotted spoon and discard. While it is reducing, season the foie gras with salt, and in a pre-heated pan add some clarified butter. Whisk in the butter. Sauté the foie gras on the BOILING PLATE until it is brown on all sides. This should take about 1½ minutes – don't overcook it. Remove with a slotted spoon to a warm plate and set aside. Check the sauce for seasoning.

5 When you are ready to serve, add the foie gras and figs to the sauce for about 1 minute, just to heat through. Place each partridge on a warmed plate and spoon over the sauce.

Conventional Cooking:
Bake the figs in the oven at 190°C/375°F/gas 5. Roast the partridges in an oven pre-heated to 220°C/425°F/gas 7.

rabbit with garlic and lemon zest
on a bed of tagliatelle

serves 6

4 tbsp olive oil	2 cloves garlic, peeled and sliced thinly
60 g white sourdough breadcrumbs	500 g tagliatelle
knob of butter	juice of ½ lemon and the zest of 1 lemon
1 kg rabbit, cut into pieces (ask your butcher or game dealer to do this for you)	1 heaped tbsp chopped rosemary
	salt and pepper

1 Put a frying pan on the SIMMERING PLATE and heat up about half the olive oil. Add the breadcrumbs and fry until they are golden. Drain them on kitchen paper and set aside.

2 In the same pan, heat the remaining oil with the butter. Add the rabbit pieces and garlic, then transfer to the floor of the ROASTING OVEN until they are cooked through and browned on all sides (this should take about 10 minutes). If necessary, add more olive oil so that the pan is not dry.

3 Meanwhile, bring a large pan of salted water to the boil on the BOILING PLATE. Add the pasta and cook until it is al dente. Drain it, leaving a little of the water in the bottom so the pasta doesn't stick together.

4 When the rabbit is cooked, transfer it to the SIMMERING PLATE and add the lemon juice and zest, rosemary and a little more olive oil if it needs it. Toss the rabbit in the pasta and arrange on warm plates, topping the rabbit and pasta with the fried breadcrumbs and a little more lemon zest for garnish.

Conventional Cooking:

This dish can be cooked in a large frying pan entirely on the hob.

venison and chestnut casserole

serves 4-6

8 juniper berries	50 g flour
800 g venison, cubed	knob of butter
3 cm piece of ginger, peeled and grated	1 large carrot, peeled and finely chopped
1 clove garlic, crushed	½ an onion, peeled and finely chopped
5 tbsp sunflower oil	250 g vacuum-packed chestnuts
100 ml red wine	salt and pepper

1 Put the juniper berries into a mortar and crack them open with a pestle to release their aroma. Put the venison, berries, ginger, garlic, 3 tbsp of oil and wine into a freezer bag and marinate the meat overnight in the fridge.

2 Season the flour with salt and pepper and remove the meat from the marinade, shaking off the excess liquid, and coat each piece in the flour.

3 Heat 2 tbsp of the oil and the knob of butter in a large casserole dish on the floor of the ROASTING OVEN and brown each piece of venison. Do not overcrowd the pan. When the meat has all been browned, add the carrot and onion to the pan and cook until they take on some colour, either on the SIMMERING PLATE or on the ROASTING OVEN floor.

4 When they are ready, add any excess flour to the pan and scrape up all the caramelised bits, then add the meat, chestnuts and finally the marinade juices. Bring it all up to the boil on the BOILING PLATE and then transfer to the SIMMERING OVEN for 2 hours or until it is tender. This can all be done the day before you want to serve it as casseroles are often better the next day. When you are ready to serve, reheat in the ROASTING OVEN for 30-60 minutes or until it is really hot, then serve with mashed potatoes.

Conventional Cooking:
Pre-heat the oven to 150°C/300°F/gas 2 and cook for 2-3 hours as above.

curried pheasant with apples and sultanas

serves 4

40 g butter	1 shallot, peeled and finely chopped
2 tbsp grapeseed oil	1 tbsp mild curry powder
2 large apples, peeled, cored, sliced into rings and dipped in lemon juice to prevent discolouring	1 tsp tomato purée
30 g golden caster sugar	30 ml game or chicken stock
15 g sultanas, soaked in hot water to cover	30 ml dry cider
4 pheasant breasts	2 tbsp crème fraîche
	salt and pepper

1 Heat half the butter and 1 teaspoon of the oil in a frying pan on the SIMMERING PLATE. Add the apple rings and sprinkle over the sugar. Fry the apples until they have caramelised in the sugar, then toss in the drained sultanas. Set aside and keep warm at the back of the Aga.

2 In a clean frying pan, add the remaining butter and oil and brown the pheasant breasts quickly on the BOILING PLATE. Transfer them to a roasting tin and roast on the third set of runners in the ROASTING OVEN for about 10 minutes. Don't overcook them or they will dry out.

3 Meanwhile, make the sauce. Pour off all but 1 tablespoon of the fat left in the frying pan and fry the shallot on the SIMMERING PLATE until it is very soft and starting to caramelise. Add the curry powder and tomato purée and cook for about 1 minute.

4 Next, pour in the stock and the cider and stir vigorously, scraping up all the caramelised bits from the bottom of the pan. Bring the sauce to the boil and reduce until it is quite thick. Season with salt and pepper. Stir in the crème fraîche. Check the seasoning.

5 When the breasts are done, cover them with foil, making sure that you rest them for at least 10 minutes in a warm place. Put a few apple rings and sultanas on each plate and pop a pheasant breast on top, then pour over a little sauce and serve with basmati rice. Hand round any remaining sauce separately.

Conventional Cooking:

Pre-heat the oven to 220°C/425°F/gas 7 and proceed as above.

crispy duck pancakes with plum sauce

This is a really easy way to cook Peking Duck at home. I've never met anyone who doesn't like it. Children love the sweet-sour flavour and adore rolling up the duck pancakes – it makes eating fun! Buy the pancakes ready made from an oriental grocer or supermarket.

serves 4 as a main course; 6 as a starter

2.3 kg oven-ready duck, dry plucked if possible
50 ml plum brandy or ordinary brandy
1 tbsp Chinese 5-spice powder
80 ml honey
1 tbsp soy sauce
1 tsp sesame oil

4 cm piece of ginger, peeled and cut into strips
200 ml hoisin sauce or plum sauce
½ a cucumber, peeled and cut into 5 cm thin strips
1 bunch of spring onions, trimmed, cut into 5 cm long strips and separated
2 x 250 g packs of Chinese pancakes

1 Deal with the duck first. You can prepare this the day before and reheat if you wish. Put the duck into a colander and pour over a kettle of boiling water to help loosen the fat. Drain the duck and dry really well with kitchen paper inside and out. Brush the duck with the brandy (alcohol helps to dry out the skin, giving a crispier finish).

2 Hang the duck up by its wings with a plate underneath in a place where there is a cool breeze (the air helps to keep the duck really dry). If this isn't possible, put it uncovered into the fridge. This can be done a day in advance, but it must be left hanging for a minimum of 6 hours.

3 When you are ready to cook the duck, put a piece of Bake-O-Glide into the half-size roasting tin and then put in the grill rack. Put the duck on the grill rack. Rub the 5-spice powder all over the bird and brush on the honey and soy sauce. Slide the tin onto the third set of runners in the ROASTING OVEN and cook for 1 hour, then transfer to the SIMMERING OVEN for a further hour or until the duck is cooked and the skin is crispy (this can take up to 2 hours). You want to end up with the meat falling away from the bones and really crispy skin.

4 While the duck is cooking, gently heat up the sesame oil and the ginger strips in a large saucepan and cook for 2 minutes on the SIMMERING PLATE. Don't burn the ginger. Remove the ginger strips and add the hoisin sauce or plum sauce and heat through. Set the sauce aside to cool.

5 When the duck has finished cooking, remove it from the oven and allow to rest for 5-10 minutes, then shred all the meat away from the carcass, cut up the skin and keep warm.

6 Follow the cooking instructions on the packaging for the pancakes and serve the shredded duck with the pancakes, cucumber and spring onion strips and the sauce. Spread some sauce over a pancake and top with some duck, spring onions and cucumber strips, roll up tightly and eat.

Conventional Cooking:
Pre-heat the oven to 200°C/400°F/gas 6 and start the duck off for about an hour, then turn down the temperature to 180°C/350°F/gas 4 and cook for another hour or so until the duck is tender.

meat

Roasting a joint of meat in the Aga is always easy and the radiant heat locks in the flavour, making it a truly different eating experience altogether. For meats like lamb and pork, you can use the slow roasting method or cook it conventionally. For good cuts of meat, veal and beef, I suggest using the fast roasting method.

Slow roasting method
Prepare the joint for cooking. Cut a couple of onions in half and put them into a tin lined with Bake-O-Glide. Put the joint on top of the onions and then slide the tin onto the fourth set of runners of the ROASTING OVEN for 30-40 minutes or until it begins to brown. Then transfer it to the SIMMERING OVEN for approximately double the amount of conventional cooking time. Weigh the joint before cooking to calculate the timings.

Conventional fast roasting method
Prepare joint as above and calculate the roasting time according to the cut and type of meat. When it is finished cooking, rest for 15-20 minutes before carving.

beef
Rare: 12 minutes per 450 g
Medium: 15 minutes per 450 g
Well done: 20 minutes per 450 g

lamb
Pink in the middle: 15 minutes per 450 g
Well done: 20 minutes per 450 g

pork
25 minutes per 450 g

veal
15 minutes per 450 g

fillet of beef

This method of cooking a whole fillet of beef gives you a beautifully rare middle.

For 900 g fillet, put about 2 tablespoons of dripping in the large roasting tin and place it on the ROASTING OVEN floor. When the fat is smoking, take the tin out, put it on the BOILING PLATE and seal the meat on all sides. The fat will splatter so you will need a damp cloth nearby. Remove the excess fat and then hang the tin on the third set of runners in the ROASTING OVEN. Cook for no more than 15-20 minutes. When the cooking time is up, take the fillet out of the oven and remove from the tin. Do not wash the tin. Wrap the meat very tightly in cling film, twisting the ends for a really snug fit. Put the fillet onto a plate and leave it to rest for at least 20 minutes on top of the protected SIMMERING PLATE. To serve the meat, remove the cling film, put the meat back into the tin and put the tin on the ROASTING OVEN floor for 8-10 minutes, just to heat it through. Serve it straight away.

herb crusted loin of lamb

serves 6

1 x 150 g loin fillet per person, trimmed

FOR THE HERB CRUST:
½ onion, peeled and cut in quarters
2 rashers of smoked streaky bacon, cut into pieces
1 clove garlic, peeled
1 tbsp fresh basil

1 tbsp fresh mint
3 tbsp soft white breadcrumbs
2 tbsp grated Parmesan cheese
2 tbsp butter, softened
salt and pepper

1 Trim the fillets of any fat and make them all roughly the same size.

2 Put all the herb crust ingredients into the bowl of a food processor and combine until thoroughly mixed together. Press the mixture on top of each fillet and place on a baking sheet lined with Bake-O-Glide. At this stage the fillets can be left in the fridge, covered, until you want to cook them.

3 Cook the fillets on the second set of runners in the ROASTING OVEN for 12-15 minutes, depending on how rare/well done you like them. Serve on a bed of mashed potatoes with courgettes sautéed in basil and mint.

Conventional Cooking:
Pre-heat oven to 220°C/425°F/gas 7 and continue as above.

grilled chump chops

serves 4

4 lamb or pork chump chops
1 clove garlic, peeled
60 g soft butter

1 tbsp chopped parsley
1 lemon, preferably organic
salt and pepper

1 Heat the Aga grill pan on the floor of the ROASTING OVEN until it is very hot.

2 While the pan is heating up, rub each chop with the garlic and season with salt and pepper. Place the grill pan on the BOILING PLATE and put in the chops. Transfer to the floor of the ROASTING OVEN for 3-4 minutes (pork will take a little longer), then turn the chops over and cook for a further 3-4 minutes.

3 Crush the garlic and mash it into the butter with the parsley and season with the juice and zest of the lemon and salt and pepper.

4 When the chops are cooked, take the grill pan out of the oven and put a small knob of the garlic butter on each chop. Rest for 5 minutes and serve with a green salad and crusty bread.

Conventional Cooking:
Heat a grill pan on the hob and cook the entire dish on hob.

gigot boulangère

This is simply lamb cooked on potatoes. The Aga cooks this dish to perfection.

serves 6

olive oil
1.8 kg potatoes, peeled and sliced thinly
2 onions, peeled and finely sliced
1 tbsp rosemary, chopped, plus some sprigs to push into the meat

100 ml white wine
4 cloves garlic
2.4 kg leg of lamb
salt and pepper

1 Line the large roasting tin with Bake-O-Glide. Drizzle a little olive oil onto the bottom and layer the potato slices, onion, chopped rosemary and salt and pepper into the tin. Pour over the white wine.

2 Cut the garlic into slivers and push them and the rosemary sprigs into the leg of lamb, making slits with a sharp knife.

3 Lay the lamb on top of the potatoes and rub in some olive oil and salt and pepper all over the lamb. Hang the tin on the third set of runners in the ROASTING OVEN and cook for 45 minutes. Transfer to the SIMMERING OVEN for 3-4 hours or until the lamb is tender. Serve with the juices from the tin.

Conventional Cooking:
Pre-heat the oven to 200°C/400°F/gas 6 and cook the potatoes for 1-1½ hours. Place the lamb on top of the potatoes and cook the lamb for 18 minutes per 500 g, depending on how well done you like your meat (about 1½ hours). Rest the meat for 10 minutes before serving.

sausages and mash

serves 6

900 g potatoes, peeled and cut in half
80 g butter
150 ml crème fraîche, double cream or sour cream

12 sausages
salt and pepper

1 Put the potatoes into a saucepan, pour in water to cover, bring to the boil on the BOILING PLATE and boil for 3 minutes. Take the pan off the BOILING PLATE and drain off all the water. Replace the lid and transfer to the SIMMERING OVEN for 20-30 minutes.

2 When the potatoes are tender, break them up with a knife and mash in the butter and crème fraîche. Season with lots of salt and pepper. If they are too stiff, add more crème fraîche or a little milk.

3 While the potatoes are cooking, put the half-size grill rack into the half-size roasting tin and lay the sausages on top. Slide the tin onto the highest set of runners in the ROASTING OVEN and cook the sausages for 20-30 minutes, turning halfway through cooking so they are coloured on all sides.

4 When the sausages are ready, serve with the mashed potatoes and gravy.

Conventional Cooking:
Cook the sausages in a frying pan on the hob.

veal cutlets with sage, thyme and garlic butter

serves 4

200 g flour, seasoned with salt and pepper
3 large eggs, beaten
300 g fresh white breadcrumbs
4 French-trimmed veal cutlets
clarified butter (see page 27)
2 lemons, halved

FOR THE SAGE, THYME AND GARLIC BUTTER:
250 g soft butter
2 cloves garlic, peeled and crushed
1 tbsp sage leaves, finely chopped
1 tbsp thyme leaves

1 First make the butter. Mash the butter with the garlic and the herbs really well in a bowl. Spoon the butter along the middle of a piece of greaseproof paper. Roll it up to form a sausage shape and twist the ends. Refrigerate for at least 1 hour or until firm.

2 Place a frying pan on the floor of the ROASTING OVEN to heat up. Meanwhile, put the flour into a shallow bowl or on a plate and the same with the beaten eggs and the breadcrumbs. Dip the veal cutlets first into the flour, then the egg, then the breadcrumbs. Repeat this so that each cutlet has a double coating of breadcrumbs.

3 Remove the frying pan when it is smoking and melt enough of the clarified butter to shallow fry in it on the SIMMERING PLATE. When it is ready, add the cutlets to the pan and transfer to the ROASTING OVEN floor for 8 minutes each side. Drain on kitchen paper, put on a warm plate and rest in the SIMMERING OVEN for 10 minutes.

4 Cut the herb butter into four rounds. Remove the veal from the SIMMERING OVEN. Put a slice of butter on each and return the cutlets to the ROASTING OVEN for about 1 minute or until the butter starts to melt. Serve each cutlet with half a lemon.

Conventional Cooking:
Cook this on the hob. Heat the grill pan until smoking and cook as above.

crackling roast pork

The secret to getting the crackling really crispy is to start off with very dry skin. If you are keeping the skin on the joint, leave it in the fridge for 24 hours, patted dry with a piece of kitchen paper and uncovered. Score it with a very sharp knife so that the cuts are only 1 cm apart.

serves 6-8

3 kg leg of pork on the bone	**FOR THE GRAVY:**
salt	1 ½ tbsp flour
3 onions	100 ml cider
100 g lard	1 litre stock or cooking water from vegetables
	1 tsp apple jelly
	salt and pepper

1 On the day before, remove the rind/skin from the pork leg with a sharp knife. Leave the skin to dry out overnight in the fridge, as above.

2 To cook, slice the pork rind/skin into strips about 2 cm thick. Melt the lard in the half-size roasting tin in the SIMMERING OVEN and add the pork skin strips to the fat. Cook in the SIMMERING OVEN for 3-4 hours or until it is translucent.

3 Move the tin to the second set of runners in the ROASTING OVEN and cook for 40-60 minutes. It should be crisp and twisted into curly shapes. Drain on kitchen paper and sprinkle liberally with salt. Store at the side of the Aga until ready to use. This can be made the day before if you like.

4 Score the fat left on the meat and cut the onions in half. Line the large roasting tin with Bake-O-Glide and stand the pork on the onions, cut side down, and cook for 2½-3 hours on the fourth set of runners in the ROASTING OVEN or until done. Cover the meat loosely with foil and rest for 15 minutes. (My preferred method for cooking this dish is to cook the pork for 45-60 minutes in the ROASTING OVEN then transfer to the SIMMERING OVEN for 3-4 hours or until done.)

5 While the meat is resting, make the gravy. Spoon away all but 2 tablespoons of fat from the tin. Do not remove the onions. Sprinkle in the flour and stir well so it absorbs all the fat. Pour in the cider and bring to the boil on the BOILING PLATE until it has almost evaporated, then pour in the stock or vegetable water (the quantity depends on how thick you like your gravy). Add the apple jelly to give a hint of sweetness. Bring the gravy to a rapid simmer on the SIMMERING PLATE and let it cook for about 5 minutes. Taste, season and reduce until it has reached the required consistency. Strain it into a jug and keep warm at the back of the Aga or in the SIMMERING OVEN. Serve the pork with the gravy and crackling.

Conventional Cooking:

To cook the rind, pre-heat the oven to 150°C/300°F/gas 2 and cook as in step 2. Then turn up the heat to 220°C/425°F/gas 7 and continue as in step 3. Roast the pork in a pre-heated oven to 220°C/425°F/gas 7 for 2½-3 hours.

braised beef

All casseroles taste much better if made one day in advance and then re-heated before serving.

serves 6-8

1 litre red wine	1 tbsp flour
200 ml port	1 tbsp mustard powder
1.2 kg braising steak, cut into large cubes	100 g beef dripping
2 sprigs of thyme, leaves removed from the stalks and stalks discarded	salt and pepper
3 red onions, peeled and quartered	

1 Bring the wine and the port up to the boil for 2 minutes in a saucepan on the BOILING PLATE, then cool. Put the beef cubes, thyme, and onions into a large plastic bag, then pour over the cooled wine and port. Marinate in the fridge for 24 hours.

2 When you are ready to cook the beef, remove it from the marinade. Reserve the marinade. Put the flour and mustard powder into a large bowl and season with salt and pepper. Toss the beef cubes in the flour mix until they are well coated.

3 Melt the dripping in a casserole and brown the meat on the floor of the ROASTING OVEN. You will have to do this in batches so as not to overcrowd the pan and so the meat browns on all sides. When all of the meat is

browned, tip in any remaining flour-mustard mix and stir so that the fat absorbs the flour. Put the meat back into the casserole and pour over the marinade.

4 Cover the casserole and bring this to the boil on the BOILING PLATE, then transfer to the ROASTING OVEN for 40 minutes. Transfer the casserole either to the BAKING OVEN if you have one and cook for 4 hours, or to the SIMMERING OVEN and cook for 5-6 hours or until the meat is tender. Serve with mashed potato.

Conventional Cooking:

Once the meat has been browned, bring it to the boil as above, then transfer to an oven pre-heated to 150°C/300°F/gas 2 and cook for 2-3 hours or until tender.

oven-roasted spare ribs

Allow a minimum of 450 g ribs per person if you want to feed lots of people.

serves 6

2.7 kg pork spare ribs, unseparated

FOR THE SAUCE:
5 cm piece of fresh ginger, grated
2 cloves garlic
80 ml honey

120 ml hoisin sauce
1 tsp Chinese 5-spice powder
2 tbsp soy sauce
1 tbsp brown sugar
1 tbsp Chinese rice wine

1 Mix all of the sauce ingredients in a large bowl. Add the ribs and marinate in the sauce in the fridge for a minimum of 1 hour, or longer if possible.

2 Drain the ribs from the marinade, reserving the sauce. Line the large roasting tin with Bake-O-Glide and lay the ribs in the tin. Hang the tin on the fourth set of runners in the ROASTING OVEN and bake for 40 minutes.

3 Pour the sauce into a saucepan and bring to the boil on the BOILING PLATE. When the ribs have been in for 40 minutes, pour the sauce over them and transfer them to the SIMMERING OVEN for 1-2 hours or until the meat is tender. Serve hot with finger bowls and lots of napkins!

Conventional Cooking:
Pre-heat the oven to 220°C/425°F/gas 7 and cook the marinated ribs for 1 hour. Turn down the heat to 150°C/300°F/gas 2. Pour over the boiled sauce and cook the ribs for 2-2½ hours.

balsamic pork roast

serves 6

2.5 kg boned pork loin, rind and fat removed
2 red onions, peeled and quartered
50 g butter
1 tbsp olive oil

1 tbsp fresh thyme leaves
350 ml balsamic vinegar
50 ml red wine
salt and pepper

1 Pre-heat an Aga cast iron grill pan on the floor of the ROASTING OVEN. Remove the pan from the oven and place it on the BOILING PLATE. Seal the pork fillet on all sides.

2 Put the onion, butter, olive oil and thyme into the large roasting tin. Place the pork in the tin and add the balsamic vinegar, making sure the meat is well coated in the onion/vinegar mixture. Slide the tin onto the third set of runners of the ROASTING OVEN and roast the pork for 45-50 minutes, turning the pork in the juices halfway through cooking. Check that the pork is cooked right through.

3 When the meat is ready, place the pork on a warm dish and leave to rest while you de-glaze the roasting tin with the red wine. Put the tin directly onto the SIMMERING PLATE and pour in the red wine. Reduce the pan juices for 4-5 minutes. Check the seasoning. Slice the pork thinly and serve accompanied by the onion balsamic jus.

Conventional Cooking:
Pre-heat the oven to 200°C/400°F/gas 6 and roast the pork for 1-1¼ hours.

right: oven-roasted spare ribs

the ultimate roasted rib of beef

The quality of the meat is of paramount importance; it is worth buying well-hung meat from a really good old-fashioned, top-quality butcher. Look for Aberdeen Angus – it is hard to beat! The cooking times for rare, medium and well-done meat are on page 80.

serves 6-8

1 tbsp beef dripping	FOR THE GRAVY:
3 kg forerib of beef on the bone	1½ tbsp flour
3 onions, unpeeled unless they are dirty, cut in half	1 glass red wine
salt and pepper	1 litre stock or vegetable cooking water

1 Put the dripping into the large roasting tin and melt in the ROASTING OVEN until it is smoking. Transfer the tin to the BOILING PLATE and seal the joint of beef in the dripping, making sure all the sides of the meat are browned. Set the meat aside.

2 Place the onions in the tin, cut side down. Stand the meat on top of the onions and season with some salt and pepper. Hang the tin on the third set of runners of the ROASTING OVEN and cook for about 1¾ hours for rare beef. Adjust the time to suit your taste.

3 Rest the meat for at least 15 minutes in a warm place (the WARMING PLATE if you have a 4-oven Aga or next to a 2-oven Aga), covered loosely with foil.

4 While the meat is resting, make the gravy. Spoon away all but 2 tablespoons of fat from the tin. Do not remove the onions. Sprinkle in the flour and stir well so it absorbs all the fat. Pour in the wine and bring to the boil until it has almost evaporated, then pour in either stock or water (the quantity depends how thick you like your gravy). Bring the gravy up to a rapid simmer on the SIMMERING PLATE and let it cook there for about 5 minutes. Taste, season and reduce until it has reached the required consistency. Strain it into a jug and keep warm at the back of the Aga or in the SIMMERING OVEN.

Conventional Cooking:
Pre-heat the oven to 220°C/425°F/gas 7 and cook as above.

toad in the hole

The jury is still out about whether one should or shouldn't let the batter stand for a few hours. To get ahead, I make my batter the day before; if I'm pushed for time, it stands for as long as it takes the fat to get up to temperature – the choice is up to you. Whatever you do, don't prick the sausages!

serves 4

8 sausages
60 g dripping
salt and pepper

FOR THE BATTER:
3 eggs
175 g plain flour
175 ml milk
110 ml water

FOR THE ROASTED ONION GRAVY:
2 medium onions, peeled and sliced
1 tsp sugar
1 tbsp sunflower oil
1 rounded tbsp flour
1 tbsp Worcestershire sauce
1 tbsp Dijon mustard
1 tsp apple jelly
1 tsp chopped sage
1 litre chicken stock
salt and pepper

1 First make the batter. Whisk the eggs and flour together, then sift in the flour and whisk, then slowly add the milk and water, whisking continuously. Season with salt and pepper. Set aside.

2 Put the half-size grill rack into the half-size roasting tin and lay the sausages on top. Slide the tin onto the highest set of runners in the ROASTING OVEN and cook the sausages for 20 minutes, turning halfway through cooking so they are coloured on all sides.

3 Remove the sausages and the grill rack from the tin. Put the dripping into the tin and heat it up in the ROASTING OVEN until it is smoking hot. Move the tin to the SIMMERING PLATE. Put the sausages back in the tin, then pour in the batter. Hang the tin on the third set of runners of the ROASTING OVEN and cook for 30-40 minutes or until the batter has risen and is golden brown.

4 To make the gravy, toss the onions with the sugar and oil in a large bowl. Line a roasting tin with Bake-O-Glide and scatter over the onions. Slide the tin onto the highest set of runners in the ROASTING OVEN and roast the onions for 10 minutes, then move to the floor of the ROASTING OVEN for another 5 minutes or until they are golden and caramelised. Remove the tin from the oven to the SIMMERING PLATE and sprinkle in the flour and stir it well to absorb all of the fat. Add the Worcestershire sauce, mustard, jelly and sage, then add the stock little by little, stirring constantly. Season, then cook for 4-5 minutes on the SIMMERING PLATE. Pour into a warmed jug and serve.

Conventional Cooking:

Cook the sausages in the usual way. Pre-heat the oven to 220°C/425°F/gas 7 and cook for 40-45 minutes. To make the gravy, pre-heat the oven to 200°C/400°F/gas 6 and roast the onions for 15-20 minutes or until they are caramelised, then finish off the gravy on the hob.

steamed steak, mushroom and horseradish pudding

If possible, use organic mushrooms as they have more flavour.

serves 6

FOR THE SUET PASTRY:	knob of butter
350 g self-raising flour	1 tbsp flour
175 g suet	600 g chuck steak, cut into cubes
cold water, to bind	185 g button mushrooms, cut in half if they are big.
salt	2 tbsp freshly grated horseradish (or jarred if fresh is not available)
FOR THE FILLING:	beef stock
1 large onion, peeled and sliced	salt and pepper
½ tbsp sunflower oil	
1 tsp caster sugar	

1 First make the pastry. Grease a 1.5 litre china pudding basin. Sieve the flour into a roomy bowl and then add the suet and a pinch of salt, mixing it in using cutting motions with a knife. Slowly add the water until you have a firmish dough. Wrap the dough in cling film and let it rest in the fridge for 30 minutes. When the pastry is ready, dust a surface with flour and roll it into a large circle, about 1 cm thick. Cut a wedge of about one-third from the circle for the lid. Carefully lift the remaining pastry and shape into a cone and fit into the pudding basin. Make a circle shape out of the reserved pastry for the lid and set aside.

2 While the pastry is resting, caramelise the onions. Put the sliced onions into a bowl and pour in the oil and sugar. Season with the salt and pepper and mix well, then tip into the half-size roasting tin, add the knob of butter and put the tin on to the floor of the ROASTING OVEN for about 20 minutes, stirring halfway through cooking. The onions should be soft and slightly charred around the edges and golden brown. Drain them and set aside. This can be done in advance.

3 Put the flour into a bowl, season with salt and pepper and toss the steak pieces in it. Add the mushrooms, horseradish and onion to the bowl and stir well to mix. Spoon the meat mix into the pudding basin and pour in enough beef stock just to cover the meat and

season with more salt and pepper.

4 Dampen the edges of the pastry with water and place the lid on top, sealing it well. Using two sheets of foil, butter the sheet that will be closest to the pastry and then cover the top of the pudding with it, making a pleat on the top to allow for expansion. Tie with string, making a handle for easy removal.

5 If you have a cake baker, use it for steaming or put a trivet into a large pot with a lid and stand the pudding on the trivet. Pour boiling water into the pot so that it comes halfway up the sides of the basin and bring the water back to the boil on the BOILING PLATE. Cover with the lid and move to the ROASTING OVEN for 30 minutes, then transfer to the SIMMERING OVEN for about 5-6 hours.

6 When the pudding is cooked, remove it from the steamer and let it rest for 10 minutes before turning out. Cut into wedges and serve.

Conventional Cooking:
Place the pudding on a trivet in a deep saucepan. Pour in enough boiling water so that it comes halfway up the side of the pan and bring to the boil. Turn down the heat to a simmer and steam the pudding for 2½-3 hours, checking the pan from time to time and topping up with boiling water if necessary.

shepherd's pie

This must be made with minced lamb from a roasted joint – if you use other mince it just isn't the same. This is the ultimate 'left-over' recipe loved by everyone.

serves 6

1 tbsp sunflower oil or clarified butter (see page 27)
1 carrot, peeled and finely chopped
1 onion, peeled and finely chopped
½ tsp rosemary, chopped
1 clove garlic (optional as this depends how much garlic was used with the roasted joint)
1 tbsp flour
750 g minced roasted lamb

1 tbsp Worcestershire sauce
1 tbsp tomato ketchup
325 ml meat juice (the best is to use any leftover gravy topped up to required amount, or you can use stock)
salt and pepper

FOR THE TOPPING:
750 g mashed potato (see page 112)

1 Melt the fat in a large pan on the SIMMERING PLATE and brown the carrot and onion. Add the rosemary and garlic, then add the flour and stir well to absorb the fat.

2 Mix in the meat, sauces and gravy and then check for seasoning. Bring the meat to a simmer, then tip the meat into a pie dish and cool slightly.

3 Spread the mashed potato over the top and rough the surface up with a fork. This can be cooked immediately, frozen in this state or refrigerated until ready to cook. If you wish, dot a few pieces of butter over the surface before cooking. Place it on the third set of runners in the ROASTING OVEN for 30-40 minutes. If the top browns too quickly, use the COLD PLAIN SHELF. Serve with peas, and more Worcestershire sauce and ketchup.

Conventional Cooking:
Pre-heat oven to 200°C/400°F/gas 6 and cook for 45-60 minutes.

persian slow-roasted shoulder of lamb

This is a delicious dish that captures the aromatic essence of Middle Eastern cooking. Serve it with a rice pilaff and home-made Aga yoghurt and mint sauce.

serves 6

1 tsp coriander seeds	juice and zest of 2 limes
½ tsp cumin seeds	2 cloves garlic, crushed
4 cardamom pods	1 heaped tbsp chopped mint
2 kg shoulder of lamb, with bone in	1 tbsp olive oil
350 ml Greek yoghurt	salt and pepper

1 First dry fry the coriander seeds, cumin and cardamom pods in a frying pan on the SIMMERING PLATE for 2 minutes. Tip the spices into a pestle and mortar and crush to release the flavours.

2 Place the lamb in a shallow dish or a large sealable plastic bag (I prefer the bag method). Mix together the yoghurt, lime juice and zest, crushed garlic and mint, then rub well into the lamb. Pour over the oil and cover the dish or close the bag. Leave to marinate overnight in the fridge. Turn meat occasionally in the marinade. If you forget to do this the night before, the minimum marinating time is 1 hour.

3 When you are ready to cook the lamb, season it with salt and place it in the small Aga roasting tin. Pour over all the marinade juices. Place the tin on the third set of runners in the ROASTING OVEN and cook for 30 minutes, then transfer to the third set of runners in the SIMMERING OVEN for 2 hours, basting occasionally. After 2 hours the meat should be tender and succulent.

4 Remove the lamb from the oven and let it rest for 10-15 minutes before carving. Pour the pan juices into a blender and whiz until smooth (the reason for this is that the yoghurt will 'split' so it looks better when whizzed up!). Check the seasoning and serve this sauce with the lamb.

Conventional Cooking:

Pre-heat the oven to 180°C/350°F/gas 4 and roast for 3-4 hours. Check the meat after 3 hours – the lamb should be very tender. Rest the lamb for 15 minutes before serving.

fish and seafood

The Aga is perfect for cooking fish as it locks in the juices at the same time as crisping up the skin. One of the amazing things about the Aga is that fish can easily be cooked in the same oven as, say, a fruit tart without the transference of smell or taste.

Poaching fish

For a whole fish, such as a salmon, use the conventional fish kettle method. Make a court bouillon by filling a fish kettle with water, herbs, peppercorns and lemon halves, then put in the whole fish. Bring to the boil on the BOILING PLATE (if the kettle is large, use the SIMMERING PLATE as well). As soon as it has boiled for 5 minutes, remove the kettle from the heat and leave the fish to cool in the liquid. This method cooks fish really well and you can forget about it while it cools.

Oven-steamed fish

Steaming fish in the Aga is easy. Lay a large piece of foil on a shallow tin and butter the inside of the foil. Lay the fish on the foil and season with herbs, lemons, salt and pepper. Spoon over 1 tablespoon of white wine or water,

and then wrap up the foil into a loose parcel, fully sealed but with enough room for steam at the top. Slide the tin onto the third set of runners of the ROASTING OVEN and cook for 10-12 minutes or until the fish is cooked to your liking. Owners of 4-oven Agas can also use the BAKING OVEN, although the fish will take slightly longer to cook.

Frying fish in the roasting oven

Pour about 2-3 cm of sunflower oil into a heavy-based shallow pan. Place the pan on the floor of the ROASTING OVEN and heat until smoking. Batter the fish or coat in breadcrumbs. Remove the pan from the oven, add the fish to the pan and return to the ROASTING OVEN floor. Fry for a few minutes on each side in the pan or until the batter or breadcrumbs are golden.

smoked fish pie

serves 6- 8

650 g smoked finnan haddock
450 ml milk
½ onion, peeled and quartered
2 kippers, skinned, boned and flaked into pieces
250 g smoked salmon trimmings, chopped into bite-sized pieces
5 cornichons, chopped
3 eggs, hard-boiled, peeled and cut into wedges
2 heaped tbsp flat-leaf parsley, chopped
zest and juice of 1 lemon, preferably organic
30 g butter

30 g flour
30 ml double cream
salt and pepper

FOR THE MASHED POTATO TOPPING:
900 g potatoes
generous knob of butter
100 ml sour cream or crème fraîche
30 g Gruyère cheese, grated
salt and pepper

1 Put the potatoes into a saucepan of salted water on the BOILING PLATE. Boil for 3-4 minutes then drain off all the water, cover with a lid and move to the SIMMERING OVEN for 30-45 minutes.

2 Lay the haddock in the large roasting tin and pour over the milk. Season with pepper and add the chopped onion. If you have any parsley stalks, throw them in too. Slide the tin onto the second set of runners in the ROASTING OVEN and cook for 10 minutes.

3 Put the flaked kippers and smoked salmon trimmings into a large deep-sided ovenproof dish, and add the cornichons, egg, parsley and lemon zest.

4 When the haddock is cooked, remove the fish from the milky liquid and strain it into a jug and reserve. When the haddock is cool enough to handle, skin and flake it into the ovenproof dish with the other fish.

5 Make the sauce. Melt the butter in a saucepan on the SIMMERING PLATE and add the flour, stirring all the time. When all the flour has been absorbed into the butter, slowly add the strained milk little by little, stirring constantly. When all the milk has been used, add the lemon juice. You should have a smooth white sauce. Pour in the cream and a little salt and pepper (not too much salt as the fish is salty). Simmer the white sauce on the SIMMERING PLATE for 3-4 minutes so that it is slightly thick and glossy.

6 When it is ready, pour it over the fish, mixing it all in well so that everything is coated with the sauce. Do this gently to avoid breaking up the flakes of fish. Set aside.

7 Make the mashed potato topping. When the potatoes are done, remove them from the oven and put them through a potato ricer or mash them by hand or use an electric hand whisk until they are creamy and fluffy. Beat in the butter and sour cream or crème fraîche and season.

8 Spread the potatoes over the fish, then sprinkle over the cheese. The pie can be made to this point 24 hours in advance and refrigerated. When you are ready to cook, put the pie into the large roasting tin and slide onto the fourth set of runners in the ROASTING OVEN and cook for 35-40 minutes. The top of the pie should be crispy and enticingly browned. (If the top is browning too much, slide the COLD PLAIN SHELF onto the second set of runners.) Serve with peas.

Conventional Cooking:
Pre-heat the oven to 180°C/350°F/gas 4 and cook the pie for 40-45 minutes or until done.

hot asian tuna salad

serves 6

8 cm piece fresh ginger, peeled and cut into thin strips

3 garlic cloves, peeled and thinly sliced

6 spring onions, trimmed and sliced

6 x 250 g tuna steaks

2 tbsp fish sauce

4 tbsp soy sauce

3 tbsp Chinese rice wine vinegar

sesame seed oil

6 heads bok choy

1 tbsp oyster sauce

1 Line the large roasting tin with foil – you will be wrapping the fish up so allow for that. Scatter half of the ginger, garlic and spring onions onto the foil. Place the tuna steaks on top, then scatter over the remaining ginger, garlic and spring onions.

2 Evenly spoon over the fish sauce, soy sauce and rice vinegar. Sparingly drizzle a tiny amount of sesame oil over, then spread the bok choy over the tuna and spoon on the oyster sauce.

3 Close the foil so that the fish is well sealed in and bake on the third set of runners of the ROASTING OVEN for 15 minutes or on the third set of runners of the BAKING OVEN for 20-25 minutes. Remove from the oven and serve the tuna on top of the bok choy and spoon over the sauce. This is good accompanied by rice.

Conventional Cooking:
Pre-heat oven to 200°C/400°F/gas 6 and cook as above.

sea bass baked with green beans and anchovies

serves 6

350 g green beans, tailed and blanched

47.5 g tin anchovies

6 x 225 g sea bass fillets, boned

juice of 3 lemons

zest of 1 lemon

1 heaped tbsp fennel tops, roughly chopped

15-20 vine cherry tomatoes

olive oil

salt and pepper

1 Blanch the green beans in boiling salted water until tender. Plunge them into iced water and drain.

2 Put a sheet of Bake-O-Glide in the large shallow baking tray and spread out the beans, put the anchovies and their oil over the beans, then lay the sea bass fillets on top of the anchovies and beans. Squeeze the lemon juice over the fish and sprinkle the zest and fennel tops over. Push the tomatoes into the gaps and drizzle the whole thing with olive oil and season with salt and pepper.

3 Slide the baking tray onto the second set of runners in the ROASTING OVEN and bake for 10-15 minutes. Serve with garlic mayonnaise and crusty bread.

Conventional Cooking:
Pre-heat the oven to 200°C/400°F/gas 6 and bake the fish in the centre of the oven for 15 minutes or until done.

right: hot Asian tuna salad

crab and cod kedgeree

This is a great dish for large numbers as it is easy to make.

serves 6-8

300 g basmati rice	30 g clarified butter (see page 27)
590 ml stock or water	2 tsp madras curry powder
300 g cod	300 g crab meat, cooked
460 ml milk	4 eggs, hard-boiled, peeled and cut into quarters
1 tbsp sunflower oil	2 tbsp flat-leaf parsley, chopped
1 onion, peeled and chopped	

1 Put the rice into a saucepan with a lid and pour in the water or stock. Bring the rice to the boil on the BOILING PLATE; cover with the lid and then move the saucepan to the floor of the SIMMERING OVEN for 20 minutes.

2 Lay the cod in the large roasting tin and pour over the milk. Slide the tin onto the first set of runners in the ROASTING OVEN and cook for 5-8 minutes. Remove the cod from the liquid. Discard the milk and skin, and flake the cod into large pieces.

3 Put the sunflower oil into a frying pan and add the chopped onion. Place the frying pan on the floor of the ROASTING OVEN and fry the onions for 5-8 minutes until they are soft and starting to char around the edges. Remove from the pan with a slotted spoon and set aside.

4 In the same frying pan, melt the clarified butter and add the curry powder and stir for a few minutes. Add the crab meat and cod and cook until heated through.

5 Remove the rice from the SIMMERING OVEN and add the fish, onions and parsley. Season to taste and mix gently to avoid breaking up the flakes of fish. Transfer the kedgeree to a warmed serving dish, top with the hard-boiled eggs and sprinkle over a little more parsley.

Conventional Cooking:
Cook the rice conventionally on top of the hob. The fish can be cooked in a frying pan over a medium heat for 6-8 minutes. The dish can be finished off on the hob as above.

roast cod with lemon and rosemary vinaigrette

serves 6

6 x 225 g cod fillets
30 g butter

FOR THE VINAIGRETTE:
juice and zest of 2 lemons

1 tbsp lemon oil (see page 105)
6 tbsp mild olive oil
1 tbsp fresh rosemary leaves, finely chopped
salt and pepper

1 Whisk up the lemon juice, lemon oil, olive oil, rosemary, salt and pepper in a bowl and set aside.

2 Line the large roasting tin with Bake-O-Glide and lay the cod fillets on it. Spoon 1 tablespoon of the vinaigrette over each piece of cod. Slide the tin onto the first set of runners in the ROASTING OVEN and cook for 5-7 minutes, depending on how thick the cod is. Move the tin to the floor of the ROASTING OVEN and cook for a further 3-5 minutes.

3 When the fish is cooked, carefully lift it out, place on a warm plate and cover to keep warm.

4 To complete the sauce, put the roasting tin on the SIMMERING PLATE and pour in the remaining vinaigrette and the lemon zest and whisk in the butter. Reduce for 1 minute, whisking all the time, and pour over the cod. Serve with rice or pasta.

Conventional Cooking:
Pre-heat the oven to 200°C/400°F/gas 6 and roast the cod in the middle of the oven for 8-12 minutes.

prawn and pumpkin curry

serves 4

1 tsp cumin seeds
1 tsp coriander seeds
3 cardamom pods, split open and seeds removed
½ tsp ground turmeric
1 tbsp clarified butter (see page 27)
2 onions, peeled and chopped
3 cloves garlic, peeled and crushed

3 cm piece of ginger, peeled and grated
1 bird's eye chilli, deseeded and finely sliced
900 g pumpkin, peeled and chopped into 3 cm chunks
400 ml tin coconut milk
1 kg tiger prawns, peeled and deveined
1 large bunch of fresh coriander, roughly chopped
salt

1 Dry fry the spices in a frying pan on the SIMMERING PLATE, then pound them to a powder with a pestle in a mortar.

2 Pour the clarified butter into a deep saucepan with a lid and put it on the ROASTING OVEN floor to melt. Add the onions, cover and cook for about 10 minutes until soft.

3 Transfer it to the SIMMERING PLATE and add the spices, salt, garlic, ginger and chilli and cook for 1 minute to release the flavours. Add the pumpkin pieces and coconut milk and bring to a rapid simmer. Transfer to the SIMMERING OVEN uncovered for 20-25 minutes or until the pumpkin is tender.

4 Bring it back to the SIMMERING PLATE and reduce for 2-3 minutes. Stir in the prawns and cook for 3-4 minutes or until they are just cooked. Take the pan off the heat, add the coriander leaves and check for seasoning. Serve with basmati rice.

Conventional Cooking:
Start the cooking on the hob over a medium heat, then turn it down to a very low heat to simmer for 30-35 minutes.

fillet of salmon with a basil, bacon and sourdough crust

Today most of the salmon we buy is farmed and can be bland. To liven it up, add this crunchy crust to make it a dish fit for a dinner party or a family supper.

serves 4

4 x 175 g salmon fillets

4 tbsp fresh sourdough breadcrumbs

1 tbsp chopped basil

1 tbsp chopped flat-leaf parsley

2 rashers smoked bacon, finely chopped

2 tbsp olive oil

salt and pepper

1 Put the salmon onto a lightly greased tray (or onto a piece of Bake-O-Glide). Combine the rest of the ingredients in a bowl and spoon on top of the salmon, pressing it on firmly.

2 Cook the salmon on the floor of the ROASTING OVEN for 5 minutes, then move to the top of the oven for a further 5-8 minutes. Serve with new potatoes and green beans tossed in a lemon and olive oil dressing.

Conventional Cooking:

Pre-heat the oven to 200°C/400°F/gas 6 and bake the fish for 10-12 minutes, then place the fish under a very hot grill for 2 minutes or until the topping is golden and crispy.

salmon wrapped in brioche

serves 8

2 x 900 g salmon fillets, skinned and boned

½ tbsp semolina

FOR THE BRIOCHE:

60 g fresh yeast

150 ml milk, at blood temperature

500 g '00' pasta flour

1 tsp salt

100 g butter, melted

2 eggs, beaten

FOR THE HERB RISOTTO:

1 onion, peeled and finely chopped

olive oil

100 g arborio rice

100 ml white wine

400 ml vegetable stock

zest and juice of 1 lemon

2 tbsp tarragon, chopped

1 tbsp dill, chopped

knob of butter

salt and pepper

1 Make the brioche dough the day before or make well ahead and freeze. Crumble the yeast into the milk and set aside for about 5 minutes. Put the flour and salt into a mixer with the dough hook in place and then add the yeast, melted butter and beaten eggs. Mix for about 10 minutes on high speed or until the dough is smooth and silky. You may need to add more flour if the dough is too sticky or a little more liquid if it is too stiff.

2 Grease the inside of a large bowl and then pop the dough into it. Cover with a clean damp tea towel and leave next to the side of the Aga to rise for 1-1½ hours or until it has doubled in size.

3 Knock it back when it has risen and then put it into a plastic bag or back into the bowl, wrap it with cling film and place it in the fridge overnight or for at least 6 hours (freeze it at this stage if you wish).

4 The risotto can also be made up to a day ahead. Soften the onion in a little of the oil in a frying pan and cook on the floor of the ROASTING OVEN until it is soft. Move the frying pan to the SIMMERING PLATE and add the rice, stirring to coat every grain in the onion and oil and cook for 2 minutes or until it starts to colour.

5 Pour in the white wine and cook, stirring constantly, until it has almost all evaporated. Add the stock and season with salt and pepper. Give it another good stir and move the pan to the grid shelf on the third set of runners of the ROASTING OVEN for 20 minutes. Halfway through cooking, give it another stir.

6 When the time is up, remove the frying pan from the oven and if it is still too liquidy, cook it off on the SIMMERING PLATE until it is still loose but not sloppy. Add the lemon juice and zest, herbs and the knob of butter. Check for seasoning. Set aside to cool, then refrigerate until it is required.

7 When you are ready to assemble and cook the whole dish, bring the dough up to room temperature and roll it out on a board into a large rectangle. Line a shallow baking sheet with Bake-O-Glide and lay the brioche dough on top. Sprinkle on a little of the semolina, then lay the first salmon fillet along the centre of the dough. Season with salt and pepper, then spread the risotto on top of the fillet.

8 Lay the second fillet on top of the risotto. Brush the pastry with milk and wrap up the salmon/risotto like a parcel, long side up and over, then short sides, using the milk as 'glue'. Turn the parcel so the seam is underneath. Using a sharp knife, make six slashes on the top.

9 Put the parcel on the fourth set of runners in the ROASTING OVEN. Cook for 20 minutes, then slide the COLD PLAIN SHELF onto the second set of runners. Continue cooking for a further 20-25 minutes or until it is golden on top.

Conventional Cooking:
Pre-heat the oven to 190°C/375°F/gas 5 and bake as above.

crab spring rolls with lemon oil

makes 10 small rolls

FOR THE SPRING ROLLS:

2 tbsp sunflower oil

4 carrots, washed and grated

3 cm fresh ginger, peeled and grated

3 spring onions, trimmed and finely sliced

1 heaped tbsp freshly chopped coriander, plus more for garnish

1 bird's eye chilli, deseeded and finely sliced

1 tbsp fish sauce

1 tsp sesame oil

250 g white crab meat, cooked and shredded

500 g packet spring roll pastry, in sheets

1 egg yolk, beaten

FOR THE LEMON OIL:

peel of 1 whole unwaxed lemon

2 stalks lemongrass

250 ml grapeseed oil

1 First make the lemon oil. Peel the skin off the lemon and put it into a saucepan, then split the lemongrass and put that in. Pour the oil over the lemon skin and lemon grass.

2 Bring to the boil on the BOILING PLATE, then transfer to the SIMMERING OVEN for 30 minutes. Remove from the oven and cover with cling film. Stand at room temperature overnight. Strain into a jar and use. The oil will last for about 1 month when stored in the refrigerator.

3 To make the spring rolls, put 1 tablespoon of the sunflower oil into a frying pan and place the pan on the floor of the ROASTING OVEN. When smoking, transfer the pan to the BOILING PLATE and quickly stir-fry the carrots, ginger, onions, coriander, chilli, fish sauce, sesame oil and crab meat for 2-3 minutes. If the heat is too high, transfer to the SIMMERING PLATE. (This can be done up to 3 days in advance if you wish.)

4 Put the remaining sunflower oil into a frying pan and place it on the floor of the ROASTING OVEN until hot and smoking.

5 Lay the spring roll pastry out on a flat surface. Cut the sheets in half and brush with beaten egg yolk all around the edges. Place a teaspoon of the crab mix 4 cm from the top of the pastry, fold the pastry over the mix tightly to remove all the air, then carry on rolling it up. Secure the end with a little more egg so it acts as 'glue'.

6 When the spring rolls are complete, take the frying pan out of the oven, add the spring rolls and 'fry' them on the floor of the ROASTING OVEN in batches, adding more oil if necessary (don't forget to bring the oil up to temperature when adding more). One tablespoon of oil is all that is needed per batch. The rolls will be cooked as soon as they are brown and crispy on the outside. Serve them on a bed of salad with a little lemon oil drizzled over the top.

Conventional Cooking:

Prepare the crab rolls as above. Using a deep fat fryer, fry the rolls in batches for 2-3 minutes or until they are golden and crispy.

scallops with peas à la française

serves 4

550 g frozen peas, or podded if using fresh	zest of 1 lemon
1 little gem lettuce	1 rounded tsp caster sugar
40 g butter	2 tbsp grapeseed oil
1 level tbsp granulated sugar	1 tbsp olive oil
4 spring onions, trimmed and sliced	12 plump shucked scallops, corals removed, rinsed and drained
1 large bunch fresh mint	a little olive oil for brushing
120 ml crème fraîche	salt and pepper
1 tbsp lemon juice	

1 First make the pea purée. Put the peas, lettuce, butter, granulated sugar, spring onions, half the mint, crème fraîche and salt and pepper into a saucepan with a lid. Bring it to a rapid simmer on the SIMMERING PLATE, then transfer to the SIMMERING OVEN for 15-20 minutes or until it is tender.

2 Put the pea mixture into a blender and whiz it up until smooth or sieve it. Set it aside and keep warm either at the back of the Aga or in the WARMING or SIMMERING OVEN.

3 Place the Aga grill pan on the floor of the ROASTING OVEN to heat up.

4 Put the lemon juice, zest, caster sugar, the remaining mint, salt and pepper into a bowl and whisk until the sugar has dissolved, then whisk in the oils to make a vinaigrette.

5 Remove the hot grill pan from the roasting oven and put it on the SIMMERING PLATE. Brush each scallop with a little olive oil and sear each one in the grill pan. Cook on each side for about 1-2 minutes, depending how thick they are. Do not overcrowd the pan. When they are cooked, place them on a warmed plate and cover loosely.

6 Dollop a large spoonful of the pea purée on the centre of each plate and arrange the scallops on top. Drizzle over the vinaigrette and serve.

Conventional Cooking:

Cook the pea purée on the hob top over a gentle heat. Pre-heat a grill pan until it is smoking and cook the scallops as above.

vegetables

Root vegetables can be cooked very successfully in the Aga and retain most of their valuable vitamins as well as their taste. Once you learn the trick of cooking your veggies this way, you will never cook them any other way.

Cook green vegetables, such as French beans, peas, mangetout, etc, in the conventional way. Bring a pan of water to the boil and cook them in salted boiling water for however long you like, then drain and serve. However, when it comes to root vegetables, such as potatoes, carrots, etc, the Aga method is by far the best. Firstly, it eliminates lots of unwanted steam in the kitchen and, secondly, it conserves valuable heat.

Aga method of cooking root vegetables

Prepare the vegetables, say potatoes, in the usual way. Peel or scrub them and put into a saucepan of salted water. Bring the saucepan to the boil on the BOILING PLATE and cook with the lid on for 4-5 minutes. Remove the pan from the heat and drain off all the water. Replace the lid and put the pan on the SIMMERING OVEN floor. The potatoes will take approximately 25-30 minutes to cook but the timing really does depend on the size of the vegetables being cooked. I usually cook carrots for about 15 minutes as I like them with a bit of a bite. The amazing thing about this method of cooking vegetables is that if for some reason the meal is delayed, the vegetables happily sit in the SIMMERING OVEN for up to 3 hours without burning. It is true to say they would be well done, but they would still be edible, neither falling apart nor burnt.

Get ahead vegetables

This is a 'tricks of the trade' tip. Restaurants have been preparing vegetables like this for years.

Get ahead green vegetables

Have ready a large bowl of water with some ice in it. Put it to one side. Cook your green vegetables for 2-3 minutes in rapidly boiling water so they are tender. Using a slotted spoon, transfer them from the boiling water straight into the bowl of iced water. This is what is meant when a recipe says to 'blanch'. The iced water stops the vegetables cooking further and helps them retain their colour. Then drain well on kitchen paper towels and put into an ovenproof dish. Brush over a little melted butter or olive oil and cover with foil. Leave in a cool place or the fridge. Vegetables can be prepared in this way 24 hours in advance.

When you want to serve them, season with salt and pepper and put the dish (still covered with foil) on the floor of the ROASTING OVEN for 15-20 minutes. Open the door and when you hear the fat spitting they should be ready. Serve immediately. You can easily do all your vegetables this way and group them together in an ovenproof serving dish.

Get ahead roast potatoes

Prepare the potatoes in the usual way: peel, parboil on the BOILING PLATE for 8 minutes, drain and fluff up by putting the lid on the pan and shaking. Put the dripping or other fat into the half- or full-size roasting tin and place on the floor of the ROASTING OVEN to heat up. When the fat is smoking, add the potatoes, baste with the fat and cook on the floor of the ROASTING OVEN for 25 minutes. Take them out of the oven, turn them over and let them cool. Cover them with foil and put aside until ready to finish off. They can be prepared up to this point 24 hours ahead of time. Do not refrigerate. Remove the foil, then put the potatoes back into the ROASTING OVEN 25 minutes before you want to serve them to finish off. Serve straight away. Timings may have to be adjusted to suit the size of the vegetables.

Drying fruit and vegetables in the Aga

This is where the 4-oven Aga really comes into its own. However, it is just as easy with a 2-oven Aga.

Slice the fruit or vegetables into 1-2 cm slices or into halves or quarters. Lay the fruit or vegetables on a shallow Aga baking tray lined with Bake-O-Glide. Slide the tray into the WARMING OVEN in a 4-oven Aga for 6-8 hours or overnight. The juicier the fruit, the longer it will take to dry out. It is best to scoop out the fleshy insides of fruits like tomatoes before slicing. In a 2-oven Aga slide the tray onto the third set of runners in the SIMMERING OVEN for 3-6 hours. Leave mushrooms whole and start them in the SIMMERING or WARMING OVEN, then transfer to the lid of the BOILING PLATE, protected by a tea towel or an Aga circular chef's pad until they are really dry. Store in an airtight bag or jar and rehydrate with boiling water when you want to use. Tomatoes and aubergines can also be stored in olive oil, either with or without herbs.

roast potatoes

serves 6

900 g potatoes, peeled and cut into roughly the same size

dripping

1 Line the large roasting tin with Bake-O-Glide and put about 2 heaped tablespoons of dripping into it. Slide it onto the ROASTING OVEN floor until it is really hot and smoking.

2 Bring the potatoes up to the boil in a saucepan of water on the BOILING PLATE and cook for 5-8 minutes or until they start to give a little around the edges. Drain off all the water and, with a lid on the saucepan, shake it so that the potatoes become roughed up on the outside.

3 Remove the tin from the oven and put it on the SIMMERING PLATE. Add the potatoes to the hot fat. Baste them and move them back to the floor of the ROASTING OVEN for about 50 minutes or until they are crisp.

Conventional Cooking:
Pre-heat the oven to 200°C/400°F/gas 6 and roast the potatoes for 1 hour.

mashed potatoes

Experiment with you mash by adding different flavours – sometimes I add a whole pack of garlic cream cheese to the mash. Or squeeze in some roasted garlic cloves and mash them all up together.

serves 4-6

900 g potatoes, peeled and cut in half
80 g butter

150 ml crème fraîche
salt and pepper

1 Put the potatoes into a saucepan of water and bring to the boil on the BOILING PLATE. Boil for 3 minutes. Take the pan off the heat and drain off all the water. Replace the lid and transfer to the SIMMERING OVEN for 20-30 minutes.

2 When the potatoes are tender, break them up with a knife or a potato ricer. Mash in the butter and crème fraîche. Season with lots of salt and black pepper. If the potatoes are too stiff, add some more crème fraîche or a little milk.

Conventional Cooking:
Boil the potatoes for 8-10 minutes over a high heat. Drain and continue as above.

baked potatoes

1 potato per person

Wash the potatoes and set them on a grid shelf on the third set of runners in the ROASTING OVEN for 45-60 minutes (the cooking time very much depends on the size of the potatoes).

warm new potatoes with pancetta and pinenuts

serves 4

750 g baby new potatoes	**FOR THE WALNUT OIL VINAIGRETTE:**
250 g pancetta, cubed	1 tbsp red wine vinegar
3 tbsp pinenuts	2 tbsp sunflower oil
1 tbsp butter	1 tbsp walnut oil
2 tbsp crème fraîche	1 tsp honey
1 bag wild rocket	1 tsp Dijon mustard
	salt and pepper

1 Place the potatoes in a large pan of salted water and bring to the boil on the BOILING PLATE for 3 minutes. Drain off all the water, cover and transfer them to the SIMMERING OVEN for about 30 minutes or until they are tender.

2 While the potatoes are cooking, make the vinaigrette by whisking all the ingredients together.

3 Fry the pancetta in a frying pan on the SIMMERING PLATE until the fat starts to run, then add the pinenuts and cook until the pancetta is crisp and the pinenuts are golden – don't let them burn. Do not wash the frying pan – just set aside.

4 When the potatoes are cooked, add the butter and crème fraîche to the potatoes and season. Spoon on all but 3 tablespoons of the vinaigrette and add the pinenuts and pancetta.

5 Divide the rocket leaves between 6 plates and top with the potatoes. Pour the reserved vinaigrette into the pan and scrape up all the juices and pour these over the plated potatoes and serve while still warm.

Conventional Cooking:

Cook the new potatoes in salted boiling water on the hob until tender, then proceed as above.

baked root vegetable crumble with cucumber dressing

serves 4

3 medium parsnips, peeled and cut into chunks
3 red onions, peeled and quartered
3 carrots, peeled and cut into chunks
1 large fennel head, cut into quarters
1 sweet potato, peeled and chopped into large chunks
2 sprigs thyme, stalks removed
60 g pancetta, cubed (optional)
olive oil
butter, for greasing dish
salt and pepper

FOR THE CRUMBLE TOPPING:

180 g ciabatta breadcrumbs
1 tsp thyme leaves
zest of ½ lemon
120 g butter
60 g feta cheese, crumbled
40 g haloumi cheese, cubed

FOR THE DRESSING:

½ cucumber, peeled, deseeded and chopped into small cubes
pinch of sugar
1 tsp white wine vinegar
1 bunch mint
1 bunch dill
200 ml Greek yoghurt

1 Put the prepared vegetables into a saucepan of water and boil for 5 minutes on the BOILING PLATE. Drain off the water and tip the vegetables and the cubed pancetta (if using) into a buttered ovenproof dish. Drizzle over some olive oil and season with salt, pepper and the thyme leaves.

2 Make the crumble topping. Put the breadcrumbs into a large bowl and add salt, pepper, thyme leaves and lemon zest. Rub in the butter. Top the root vegetables with the crumble, then scatter over the cheese.

3 Put the crumble onto the fourth set of runners in the ROASTING OVEN and bake for about 40-45 minutes.

Place the COLD PLAIN SHELF on the second set of runners after 20-25 minutes.

4 While the crumble is cooking, make the dressing. Put the chopped cucumber, salt, pepper, sugar and white wine vinegar into a bowl and leave to stand for 5-10 minutes. Drain off any excess liquid, then add the herbs and yoghurt and mix well. Remove the crumble from the oven and serve with the dressing and a green salad.

Conventional Cooking:

Pre-heat the oven to 200°C/400°F/gas 6 and bake the crumble for 45-60 minutes.

dauphinoise potatoes

serves 4-6

2 cloves of garlic, peeled and crushed

15 g butter, plus more for greasing the tin or ovenproof dish

900 g potatoes, peeled and sliced very thinly

150 ml crème fraîche

425 ml double cream

salt and pepper

1 Put the garlic and butter into a bowl and gently melt and infuse at the back of the Aga. You can melt it in a saucepan if time is short but do not let the butter brown or the garlic burn.

2 Grease an ovenproof dish with some butter, then layer the potato slices in the dish.

3 Stir the garlic-infused butter into a bowl containing the two creams to lightly loosen them. Season the creams with salt and pepper. If the cream is too stiff, loosen it with a little milk. Pour the cream over the potatoes and season with more salt and pepper.

4 Slide a grid shelf onto the third set of runners in the ROASTING OVEN and cook the potatoes for 1-1½ hours. If browning too quickly, slide the COLD PLAIN SHELF in above it.

Conventional Cooking:

Pre-heat the oven to 200°C/400°F/gas 6 and bake for 1½ hours or until it is lightly coloured on top and the potatoes are tender.

stir-fried mushrooms

serves 4

2 tbsp peanut oil

500 g mixed mushrooms, such as oyster, button and shiitake

2 spring onions, trimmed and finely sliced

2 cloves garlic, peeled and thinly sliced

1 tbsp soy sauce

2 tbsp oyster sauce

2 tbsp dry sherry

1 tsp sugar

salt and pepper

1 Heat the oil in a deep-sided frying pan or wok until it is smoking on the BOILING PLATE or on the floor of the ROASTING OVEN.

2 Add the mushrooms to the pan, stirring all the time. Then add the spring onions and garlic. Stir, then toss in the rest of the ingredients and cook for 2-3 minutes. Serve straight away with rice or noodles.

Conventional Cooking:

Cook in a wok over a high heat on the hob.

vichy carrots

serves 4

700 g carrots	30 g butter
1 tbsp brown sugar	salt and pepper

1 Clean the carrots and cut them into rounds, batons or, if they are small enough, leave them whole. Put them into a saucepan and cover with water. Bring to the boil on the BOILING PLATE for 3 minutes.

2 Drain off all the water, then add the sugar, butter, salt and pepper. Cover with a tightly fitting lid and transfer to the SIMMERING OVEN for 15-20 minutes.

Conventional Cooking:
Cook the carrots in a saucepan on the hob.

sautéed courgettes with basil and mint

serves 6

700 g courgettes	1 bunch mint, chopped
40 g butter	salt and pepper
1 bunch basil, chopped	

1 Using a vegetable peeler, peel the courgettes into long thin strips.

2 Melt the butter in a large frying pan or shallow casserole on the SIMMERING PLATE until it starts to bubble, then add the courgettes, salt and pepper. Cook for about 2-3 minutes and when they start to soften, add the basil and mint. Toss for a few minutes until tender and serve.

Conventional Cooking:
Cook on a hob over a medium heat as above.

baked pumpkin with cream and gruyère cheese

serves 6 as a starter or 4 as a main course

1 medium pumpkin (about 2.5 kg)	freshly grated nutmeg
200 g tin sweetcorn	25 g butter
500 g Gruyère cheese	200 g pancetta, cubed
500 ml double cream	salt and pepper

1 Cut off the top of the pumpkin one-quarter of the way from the top. Scoop out the seeds and remove the stringy surrounding fibres. Place the pumpkin on a deep-sided baking tray.

2 Drain the sweetcorn and tip it into the pumpkin; season with salt and pepper. Add the cheese to the sweetcorn and pour over the cream. Season with more salt and pepper and a good grating of nutmeg. Throw in the butter and top with the lid.

3 Cover the whole pumpkin with foil and bake on the fourth set of runners in the ROASTING OVEN for 1½-2 hours, depending on the size of the pumpkin.

4 Meanwhile, fry the pancetta cubes in olive oil in a frying pan on the BOILING PLATE until crispy. Set aside.

5 Take the foil off the pumpkin for the last 15 minutes of cooking and test for doneness by removing the lid and inserting the point of a knife. It should be tender. Remove the lid and stir gently, taste for seasoning. then scatter over the crispy pancetta and replace the lid.

6 Take the pumpkin to the table and scoop the flesh and the creamy, cheesy goo into soup bowls. Serve piping hot with lots of crusty bread.

Conventional Cooking:
Pre-heat the oven to 200°C/400°F/gas 6 and bake the pumpkin for 2 hours.

lentils with pinenuts, lemon and mint

serves 4

500 g Puy lentils	1 bunch fresh mint, chopped
100 g pinenuts, toasted	zest and juice of 1 unwaxed lemon
2 tbsp good olive oil	salt and pepper

1 Put the lentils into a saucepan of cold water. Bring to the boil on the BOILING PLATE and add salt. Cover and transfer the lentils to the floor of the SIMMERING OVEN for 20 minutes – they should be tender but not mushy.

2 While they are cooking, toast the pinenuts in a dry frying pan on the SIMMERING PLATE and set aside.

3 Drain the lentils and put them into a warmed bowl. Pour the olive oil over and add the chopped mint, lemon juice and zest and pinenuts and toss well. Check the seasoning and serve.

Conventional Cooking:
Cook the lentils on a hob as above.

baked parsnips with apples

serves 4

675 g parsnips, peeled and cut into large chunks	30 g butter
1 large cooking apple	1 tsp golden caster sugar
juice of 1 lemon	salt and pepper

1 Bring the parsnips to the boil in a pan of water on the BOILING PLATE for 3 minutes. Drain off all the water, cover and transfer to the floor of the SIMMERING OVEN for 20-25 minutes or until very soft.

2 While the parsnips are cooking, peel and thinly slice the apple. Toss it in the lemon juice to stop it turning brown.

3 When the parsnips are tender, mash them with the butter and season with salt and pepper. Spread half of the parsnip mash over the bottom of a buttered ovenproof gratin dish, then layer the apple slices on top of the parsnips. Repeat and arrange the remaining apple slices neatly on top. Sprinkle the caster sugar over.

4 Bake on the fourth set of runners in the ROASTING OVEN for 25-35 minutes or until the apples are golden. If the apples brown too much, slide in the COLD PLAIN SHELF. For 4-oven Aga owners, cook on the third set of runners in the BAKING OVEN for 40-45 minutes.

Conventional Cooking:
Cook the parsnips as described above, then bake the dish in an oven pre-heated to 200°C/400°F/gas 6 for 30-35 minutes.

lemon and thyme potato gratin

serves 4-6

30 g butter, plus more for greasing gratin dish

900 g potatoes, thinly sliced

1½ tsp fresh thyme

the finely grated zest of an unwaxed lemon

235 ml whole milk

salt and pepper

1 Brush a gratin dish with some melted butter, next layer the potatoes, herbs, lemon zest, salt and pepper in the dish until all the ingredients are used up, finishing off with some of the herbs, lemon zest and seasoning on the top. Pour over the milk.

2 Cook on the third set of runners in the ROASTING OVEN for 35-45 minutes or until the potato is tender and the top is nicely browned.

Conventional Cooking:
Pre-heat the oven to 200°C/400°F/gas 6 and cook for 40-45 minutes.

braised red cabbage

serves 4

100 g duck fat

500 g red cabbage, thinly sliced

2 apples, peeled and grated

100 g brown sugar

250 ml red wine

250 ml port

salt and pepper

1 Melt the duck fat in a large casserole dish on the SIMMERING PLATE and add the sliced cabbage. Soften the cabbage for 5-10 minutes, then add the grated apples and brown sugar. Season with salt and pepper.

2 Pour in the wine and port and bring to the boil on the BOILING PLATE for about 2 minutes. Transfer the casserole to the floor of the SIMMERING OVEN, uncovered, for 20-30 minutes. Check the cabbage, then cover with a lid and leave to braise for 1½-2 hours or until it is soft, dark and delicious.

Conventional Cooking:
Cook the cabbage on the hob in the usual way. Turn down the heat to simmer for 30 minutes, checking and stirring from time to time.

roasted garlic

I sometimes squeeze a garlic clove into a baked potato and season with salt, pepper and a drizzle of olive oil.

per person:

1 head of garlic   **olive oil**

1 Peel away the top 2-3 layers of skin from each garlic head. Place each garlic head on a piece of foil, drizzle over the olive oil and wrap each head loosely in the foil. Place the wrapped garlic on a baking tray or in an ovenproof dish.

2 Bake the garlic in the ROASTING OVEN, on the third set of runners, for 20-30 minutes or until the garlic is soft and tender. For 4-oven Aga owners, the BAKING OVEN can also be used (bake for 45-60 minutes). Remove foil from the garlic heads and serve.

Conventional Cooking:

Pre-heat the oven to 220°C/425°F/gas 7 and roast the garlic for 1 hour.

roasted winter vegetables with rosemary and thyme

The method for roasting vegetables is the same for all vegetables except you may have to change the timings. For example, peppers take less time than root vegetables. If you wish, add garlic to the vegetables or any other herbs.

serves 6

6 baby carrots or small carrots cut into roughly the same size
3 potatoes, washed and cut into wedges (don't peel)
3 red onions or banana shallots, outside paper removed, cut through the root into quarters
½ swede, peeled and cut into chunks

½ tbsp chopped rosemary leaves
½ tbsp thyme leaves
3-4 tbsp olive oil
a pinch of sugar
salt and pepper

1 Tip all the ingredients into a large bowl or plastic bag and toss really well so that all the vegetables are well coated in the oil and herbs.

2 Line the large roasting tin with Bake-O-Glide and tip in the coated vegetables. Slide the tin onto the first set of runners of the SIMMERING OVEN and roast for 30 minutes.

3 Transfer the tin to the floor of the ROASTING OVEN for another 10 minutes or until the vegetables are tender and slightly charred.

Conventional Cooking:

Pre-heat the oven to 220°C/425°F/gas 7 and roast the vegetables for 40-45 minutes.

right: roasted garlic

aga polenta

serves 4

1 tsp sea salt	**120 g quick cook polenta**
3 tbsp olive oil	**120 g Parmesan cheese, finely grated**

1 Bring a pan of 500 ml water to the boil on the BOILING PLATE and add the salt and olive oil. Next pour in the polenta and stir well.

2 Transfer to the SIMMERING PLATE and cook for about 1 minute, then put a lid on the pan and place on the floor of the SIMMERING OVEN for 15-20 minutes or until the mixture is very thick and dense. Beat in the Parmesan. Spread out onto a flat surface, such as a plate lined with Bake-O-Glide, and let it cool completely. All this can be done up to a day in advance.

3 When you are ready to grill your polenta, cut it into wedges and heat a grill pan on the floor of the ROASTING OVEN. When the pan is really hot brush a little olive oil over the polenta wedges, take pan out of the oven, place on the BOILING PLATE and grill each side for about 2-3 minutes until they are crispy and brown. Serve with Roasted Vegetables (see page 122) and shavings of Parmesan.

Conventional cooking:
Follow the instructions on the packet of polenta. Use a very hot grill pan to grill the polenta.

aga rice

This is the easiest method of cooking rice I know of and once you try it you won't cook rice any other way! It is entirely up to you whether you rinse the rice. As a general rule, use just under double the amount of liquid to rice. To make knockout rice, fry an onion in a little oil and butter until soft then add the rice, stirring well to coat every grain with the oil/butter. Pour in home-made stock and season with salt and pepper. Cook as below. When the rice is ready, stir in a generous knob of butter.

serves 4

235 g rice	**1 tsp salt**

1 Put the rice, 370 ml water and the salt into a large saucepan and bring it up to the boil on the BOILING PLATE.

2 Stir it once, then cover with a lid and put it on the floor of the SIMMERING OVEN for 18-20 minutes.

3 Remove it from the oven, take the lid off and fluff up with a fork and cover the pan with a clean tea towel to absorb some of the steam, then serve. Brown rice will take longer: 30-40 minutes.

Conventional Cooking:
Cook as usual on the hob.

baked corn-on-the-cob with roasted garlic butter

Corn cooked this way retains all of its sweetness and goodness. This is so easy you will never boil corn again. Do use freshly picked ears if possible. The quantity of corn on the cob depends on the number of people you are feeding.

Place the grid shelf on the floor of the ROASTING OVEN. With the husks still on, put the ears of corn onto the grid shelf. Cook for about 20-25 minutes. You can stack the ears but they will take a little longer and they cook more evenly in a single layer. Serve with Roasted Garlic Butter (see below) and lots of napkins!

Conventional Cooking:
To cook conventionally, bring a large pan of water up to the boil, add salt, drop in the corn ears (husk removed) and cook for about 15 minutes.

roasted garlic butter

serves 8

2 whole garlic heads, with the tops sliced off so that the raw cloves are exposed; do not separate the cloves.
2 tbsp good olive oil

250 g butter, at room temperature
salt and pepper

1 Lay out a large piece of foil, put the garlic heads on top and drizzle over the olive oil. Wrap the foil around the garlic tightly and put on to a baking tray. Put it into the ROASTING OVEN for 20-30 minutes or until the garlic cloves are soft.
2 Put the butter, salt and pepper into a bowl. When the garlic is cooked, set aside to cool. When it is cool enough to handle, squeeze the cloves to release the pulp onto the butter and mash it all together. Transfer to a bowl and keep in the fridge until you are ready to serve. This will keep for up to 2 days in the fridge.

Conventional Cooking:
Pre-heat oven to 220°C/425°F/gas 7 and cook for 1 hour.

puddings

Puddings come in a variety of forms from cool, fresh and exciting to warm, luscious and comforting. They are the climax to the meal; you choose the dessert to fit the mood!

tarte tatin

This is classically made with apples but you can use almost any fruit you like. Very soft fruit is not suitable and fruits such as plums and apricots will take longer to caramelise because of their juices. A good mix is quinces with apples. However, the quinces do need to be poached in sugar and water for a good 45 minutes in the SIMMERING OVEN before being used. Traditionally puff pastry is used, but this dish works just as well with home-made shortcrust. Treat yourself to a tarte tatin dish or use a heavy-bottomed frying pan. The tart can be made up to the cooking part and kept refrigerated until you are ready to bake it, or cook it early in the day and serve at room temperature.

serves 8

10-12 Granny Smith apples, peeled, cored and cut into quarters
150 g best-quality bought puff pastry
60 g unsalted butter, diced
100 g golden caster sugar
½ tsp cinnamon (optional)
pinch of cloves (optional)

FOR THE CARAMEL:
75 g golden caster sugar
30 g unsalted butter

1 First make the caramel. Place the golden caster sugar in the bottom of the tart tin and heat it on the SIMMERING PLATE until it turns a dark caramel colour. Take great care not to burn it. Remove it from the heat and stir in the butter and let it cool for a few minutes.

2 Arrange the apple quarters on the caramel, packing them in very tightly. Mix the sugar with the spices and sprinkle over the apples, then dot the butter around.

3 Roll out the pastry large enough to cover the tin. Drape the pastry over the fruit and loosely tuck it in. There needs to be room for steam to escape so the pastry doesn't go soggy.

4 Put the tart on the floor of the ROASTING OVEN for 10 minutes, then move it to the fourth set of runners and bake for 30-40 minutes. If the pastry is browning too quickly, slide the COLD PLAIN SHELF onto the second set of runners. The tart should be golden, the fruit tender and the juices caramelised. If you think the juices are not sufficiently caramelised, put the tart back on the floor of the ROASTING OVEN for a few more minutes.

5 When the tart is ready, remove it from the oven and let it stand for 5-10 minutes before turning out. Place a plate on top of the tart tin and invert. Serve with lots of double cream or vanilla ice cream.

Conventional Cooking:
Make the caramel on a hob over a medium-high heat. Add the apples to the pan and cook for 10 minutes. Continue as above and cook the tart in an oven preheated to 200°C/400°F/gas 6 for 40-45 minutes or until the pastry is golden and cooked.

roasted plums with a crunchy nutty flapjack topping

serves 6

750 g ripe plums, halved and stoned
75 g unsalted butter, plus extra for greasing dish
75 g runny honey

60 g rolled oats
50 g hazelnuts, roasted and chopped
25 g brown sugar

1 Place the plum halves in a shallow, buttered oven-proof dish.

2 Melt the butter and honey in a pan on the SIMMERING PLATE, then mix in the oats and nuts. Scatter the flapjack mix over the plums and sprinkle over the sugar.

3 Bake on the third set of runners in the ROASTING OVEN for 15-20 minutes, then transfer to the third set of runners in the SIMMERING OVEN for another 25-30 minutes. Four-oven aga owners can use the BAKING OVEN and cook the dish for 35-40 minutes. Serve with lots of whipped double cream and more brown sugar.

Conventional Cooking:

Pre-heat the oven to 180°C/350°F/gas 4 and cook for 35-40 minutes.

meringues

As a variation, try adding chocolate chips to the meringue mix once all the sugar has been added.

makes 8 large meringues

½ a lemon
4 egg whites

225 g caster sugar

1 Before you start, make sure your bowl and whisk are scrupulously clean. Rub a lemon half over the whisk and around the inside of the bowl. Line a baking tray or the COLD PLAIN SHELF with Bake-O-Glide.

2 Put the egg whites into the bowl and start to whisk the egg whites on a medium speed, increasing the speed steadily to high as you go. First the whites will bubble and turn frothy, then they will form into soft floppy peaks, and finally they will stiffen up to the stiff peak stage.

3 Add the sugar one spoonful at a time until all the sugar is used up. Spoon dollops of the meringue onto the lined plain shelf or baking tray. Slide the shelf onto the fourth set of runners in the SIMMERING OVEN for 1½-2 hours. If you like your meringues very dry, when you remove them from the oven, turn each meringue on its side and place the shelf on the SIMMERING PLATE lid, protecting it with a tea towel. Leave to dry out for another 45-60 minutes.

Conventional Cooking:

Cook the meringues in a low oven, 120°C/250°F/gas ½ for 1 hour or until dry.

panattone pudding

serves 6

255 ml milk
255 ml double cream
1 vanilla pod, split
25 g caster sugar
4 egg yolks
butter, for greasing dish

500 g panattone loaf, cut into 1 cm thick slices and then into triangles
200 ml mascarpone cheese
1 tsp vanilla extract
1 tbsp icing sugar

1 Put the milk, cream, vanilla pod and caster sugar into a saucepan and heat to just a simmer on the SIMMERING PLATE.

2 Beat the egg yolks in a large bowl, then whisk in the warm milk vigorously so that the eggs do not curdle. Set aside.

3 Butter a baking dish and cover the bottom with half the panattone slices. Pour over half of the custard, then add the rest of the panattone and the remaining custard. Cover the dish with cling film and gently press down to soak the bread thoroughly. Set aside for 20 minutes.

4 Remove cling film, place the baking dish in another larger roasting tin and pour in hot water to come halfway up the sides of the baking dish. Slide the tin onto the fourth set of runners of the ROASTING OVEN and bake for 20 minutes until just set.

5 Beat the mascarpone cheese with the vanilla extract and icing sugar. If it is too stiff, add a little milk to loosen. Remove the pudding from the oven and serve warm with the sweetened mascarpone.

Conventional Cooking:

Pre-heat the oven to 200°C/400°F/gas 6. Put the pudding dish in a large roasting tin and pour boiling water into the tin to come halfway up the sides of the dish and bake for 20 minutes.

lemon verbena baked custard

serves 6

700 ml milk
3 vanilla pods
170 g caster sugar

4 lemon verbena teabags
6 large eggs

1 Pour the milk into a saucepan. Cut the vanilla pods down the centre and scrape out the seeds from the middle using the back of a knife or a spoon. Add the seeds to the milk with the sugar and lemon verbena teabags.

2 Bring the milk to the boil on the BOILING PLATE, then take it off the heat and leave the milk to infuse for 15 minutes.

3 Whisk the eggs in a large bowl. Remove the teabags from the milk, then slowly whisk the milk into the eggs. Strain the custard into six ramekins.

4 Fold a tea towel in half and place it on the bottom of the large roasting tin. Put the ramekins on the tea towel and pour boiling water into the tin to come halfway up the sides of the ramekins.

5 Bake the custards on the third set of runners in the ROASTING OVEN for about 15 minutes or until they are just set, or on the third set of runners in the BAKING OVEN for 20 minutes. Remove the ramekins from the water bath and leave to cool. Cover with cling film and refrigerate. Bring to room temperature before serving.

Conventional Cooking:
Pre-heat the oven to 180°C/350°F/gas 4 and bake for 20 minutes or until just set.

lemon pudding

You will need an electric mixer or very strong arms for this recipe!

serves 6

100 g unsalted butter, room temperature
185 g golden caster sugar
4 large eggs, separated
40 g plain flour

400 ml milk
juice of 3 lemons
zest of 2 lemons

1 Cream the butter and sugar together until they are light and fluffy. With the machine still running, add one egg yolk at a time, followed by the flour and milk, then the lemon juice and zest. The batter should be light and cake-like.

2 In a clean bowl, whisk the egg whites to the stiff peak stage and fold in the batter. Pour the mix into a large, lightly greased pudding basin.

3 Set the basin on the trivet in the cake baker. (If you do not have a cake baker, use a deep-sided saucepan large enough to take the pudding basin.) Pour in boiling water to come halfway up the side of the basin and bring the whole thing to the boil on the BOILING PLATE. Transfer it to the floor of the SIMMERING OVEN for 2 hours or until it is spongy, puffed up and golden on top.

4 Serve the pudding in bowls, making sure everyone gets some of the juices at the bottom, and with lots of thick double cream.

Conventional Cooking:
Steam on the hob over a low heat so that the surrounding water is at a gentle simmer. Check the water from time to time and top up with boiling water if necessary.

soft fruit soufflé

People think soufflés are really difficult but in fact most of the work can be done a few days in advance, leaving only the egg whites to be whisked! Do not use this method with citrus fruits. A spicy apple and cinnamon purée also works well. Fruit chunks can be added to the bottom of the mould before filling, if you wish.

serves 4

FOR THE FRUIT BASE:
350 g soft fruit, such as raspberries or strawberries
75 g caster sugar
25 g cornflour
1 egg yolk

FOR THE MERINGUE:
6 egg whites
40 g caster sugar

2 tbsp unsalted butter, for greasing moulds
4 tbsp caster sugar, for dusting moulds

1 To make the fruit base, put the fruit and 75 g caster sugar into a saucepan with 50 ml water and bring to the boil on the BOILING PLATE. Continue to boil for 2 minutes. Take off the heat and liquidise, strain and then put it back into a saucepan. If you use bought fruit purée, measure out 360 g.

2 Mix the cornflour with 3 tablespoons of water in a bowl to make a thin paste.

3 Put the pan with the fruit base on the SIMMERING PLATE and start whisking the fruit purée and add the cornflour paste little by little, whisking continuously until the mixture thickens. Take off the heat, and, still whisking, add the egg yolk. The consistency should be that of clotted cream. Set aside until ready to use. (Up to this point, the whole process can be made in advance and stored in the fridge for up to 3 days. When you take it out of the fridge, gently warm the fruit mixture through so that it comes back to the clotted cream consistency.)

4 Grease four china ramekins very generously with unsalted butter, paying particular attention to the lip of the moulds. Sprinkle a tablespoon of caster sugar into the moulds and swirl it round to lightly dust the inside, making sure the moulds are well coated. Set on a baking sheet ready to fill.

5 In a mixer with a scrupulously clean bowl, whisk the egg whites until stiff. Add the 40 g caster sugar spoonful by spoonful until it is all used up. Fold a large dollop of the meringue into the fruit purée to loosen the mix. Gently fold in the rest of the egg whites until thoroughly blended and there are no pockets of white showing.

6 Fill the prepared moulds to the top with the soufflé mixture and run a clean finger around the lip to form a neat edge. Transfer the soufflés back to the baking sheet and slide the baking tray onto the fourth set of runners in the ROASTING OVEN and bake for 5-7 minutes. Serve directly from the oven.

Conventional Cooking:
Pre-heat the oven to 180°C/350°F/gas 4 and cook for 8 minutes.

glazed passionfruit tart

serves 6

225 g caster sugar

5 eggs

2 egg yolks

170 ml passionfruit juice (sieve fresh passionfruits to give the required amount), plus more for garnishing

160 ml whipping cream

deep 23 cm tart tin lined with sweet pastry (see below) and blind-baked until golden

icing sugar, for glazing

1 Put the caster sugar, eggs, egg yolks, passionfruit juice and cream into a bowl, place it over a pan of simmering water on the SIMMERING PLATE and cook until the mixture reaches 80°C on a thermometer (or, if you don't have a thermometer, until the mixture coats the back of a wooden spoon; the main thing to avoid is the mix boiling as it will split and be unusable).

2 Pour it into the baked pastry case. Put the tart on a baking dish so taking it in and out of the oven will be easy.

3 Cook the tart on the third set of runners in the SIMMERING OVEN for 10-12 minutes. It should still have a little bit of a wobble so don't overcook it.

4 Leave to cool completely, then cut into required portions and dust with the icing sugar and glaze with a blowtorch. Slice open a passionfruit and dribble the juice – pips and all – around each slice of tart.

Conventional Cooking:
Pre-heat the oven to 120°C/250°F/gas ½ and bake for 10-15 minutes.

sweet pastry

this makes enough to line 2 tart tins

170 g icing sugar

4 egg yolks

255 g unsalted butter, at room temperature

1 tsp baking powder

pinch of salt

520 g plain flour

4 tbsp cold water

1 Mix together the sugar, egg yolks, soft butter, baking powder and salt in a large bowl.

2 Sift the flour onto the buttery mixture and, using your fingers, rub it all together until it has a sandy texture. Add the water and quickly press it into soft dough (it is easiest to tip it all onto a clean work surface and mix it together).

3 Wrap the dough in cling film and refrigerate overnight or for a minimum of 4 hours before using. The raw pastry freezes very well.

right: glazed passionfruit tart

cheesecake

serves 6-8

FOR THE BASE:

200 g digestive biscuits, smashed into crumbs

50 g chopped hazelnuts

60 g butter, melted

FOR THE TOPPING:

175 g caster sugar

400 g cream cheese

285 ml sour cream

3 large eggs

1 vanilla pod, seeds scraped out

fresh strawberries

1 Mix the digestive crumbs, nuts and butter in a bowl and press into a 20 cm spring form tin. Cover with cling film and refrigerate until set, about 45 minutes.

2 Using a mixer, blend the sugar, cream cheese, sour cream, eggs and vanilla seeds together and pour onto the prepared biscuit base. Set a grid shelf on the floor of the ROASTING OVEN.

3 For 4-oven Aga owners, start the cake on the grid shelf on the floor of the ROASTING OVEN for 10 minutes. Move the cheesecake to a grid shelf on the floor of the BAKING OVEN and cook for a further 1-1½ hours. If it browns too quickly, slide the COLD PLAIN SHELF over the cake.

4 For 2-oven Aga owners, start the cake on the grid shelf on the floor of the ROASTING OVEN for 20 minutes with the COLD PLAIN SHELF directly above it. Remove the cake and plain shelf from the ROASTING OVEN and transfer the plain shelf to the third set of runners in the SIMMERING OVEN. Place the cake on the plain shelf and continue cooking for 1½-2 hours, checking every so often.

5 Remove the cheesecake from the oven and allow to cool. Refrigerate for a few hours before serving, then serve with a topping of fresh strawberries.

Conventional Cooking;

Pre-heat the oven to 150°C/300°F/gas 2. Bake in the centre of the oven for 30 minutes, then turn off the oven and leave the cheesecake to cool completely in the oven.

banana, peach and rum crumble

I make no apologies for the tinned peaches! This recipe makes a lot of crumble mix. If you do not use all of the topping, freeze it for another time.

serves 6-8

FOR THE FILLING:
6-8 ripe bananas, peeled
450 g tin peaches in syrup
35 ml rum

FOR THE CRUMBLE TOPPING:
350 g plain flour
235 g butter
118 g brown sugar, plus a little more for the final topping

1 Butter an ovenproof dish. Slice the bananas and arrange at the bottom of the dish. Drain the peaches, reserving about 2 tablespoons of the syrup, and put them in with the bananas. Pour over the rum and the reserved syrup and set aside.

2 In a roomy bowl, sift in the flour and rub in the butter. When the mix resembles coarse breadcrumbs, mix in the sugar. Spoon the crumble topping over the fruit and sprinkle over some more brown sugar.

3 Put the dish into an Aga roasting tin and hang the tin on the fourth set of runners in the ROASTING OVEN and cook for 20-25 minutes, then transfer to the second set of runners in the SIMMERING OVEN and cook for a further 20-25 minutes or until the fruit is tender and the topping is cooked. For 4-oven Aga owners, use the third set of runners in the BAKING OVEN and cook for 35-45 minutes. Serve the crumble with lots of thick double cream.

Conventional Cooking:
Pre-heat the oven to 180°C/350°F/gas 4 and bake the crumble for 30-40 minutes.

coconut rice pudding

serves 4-6

Unsalted butter, for greasing
120 g pudding rice
60 g caster sugar

600 ml milk
600 ml coconut milk

1 Grease a large ovenproof dish with unsalted butter. Add all the ingredients to the ovenproof dish and stir well to combine.

2 Put the dish on the third set of runners in the ROASTING OVEN for 20-25 minutes, or in the BAKING OVEN if you have a 4-oven Aga for 25-30 minutes, or until a skin has formed and the pudding is starting to turn golden on top.

3 Take the pudding out and stir, then transfer the dish to the third set of runners in the SIMMERING OVEN for 2½ hours or until the pudding is cooked.

Conventional Cooking:
Pre-heat the oven to 150°C/300°F/gas 2. Cook the pudding in the centre of the oven for 30 minutes. Stir, then continue cooking for 1½ hours.

baked apples with marzipan and calvados

serves 6

125 g marzipan, chopped into small pieces

2 tbsp apricot jam

150 g dried figs, chopped into small pieces

6 apples (Granny Smiths are ideal), cored and scored horizontally around the middle with a knife

100 ml Calvados

50 ml pure apple juice

150 g brown sugar

28 g unsalted butter

crème fraîche, to serve

1 Mash the marzipan, apricot jam and figs together in a bowl and stuff each apple core generously with the mix. Place the apples in the half-size roasting tin lined with Bake-O-Glide.

2 Put the Calvados, apple juice, sugar and butter into a saucepan and bring to the boil on the BOILING PLATE and cook for 2-3 minutes. Pour the syrup over the apples.

3 Slide the tin onto the third set of runners of the ROASTING OVEN and bake for 30-35 minutes or until the apples are tender but still hold their shape. If the apples are browning too much, move them to the fourth set of runners and slide the COLD PLAIN SHELF onto the second set of runners. For 4-oven Aga owners, bake in the BAKING OVEN for 40-45 minutes.

4 Serve the apples on warmed plates with the syrup spooned over and crème fraîche.

Conventional Cooking:

Pre-heat the oven to 200°C/400°F/gas 6 and bake the apples for 40-45 minutes or until they are tender.

baking

Baking in the Aga is easy once you know how. Baking bread is fantastic because the Roasting Oven in an Aga is just like a baker's oven. Anything to do with pastry is a science and the trick is to be precise with all the measurements. Throughout my experiences as an Aga demonstrator, the most requested recipes are anything to do with baking – one of the great mysteries to Aga owners seems to be the Victoria Sponge (see page 146). I am willing to bet this chapter will be well thumbed and referred to often. Use the recipes as a guide when adapting your own baking recipes.

Baking is where the Cold Plain Shelf comes into its own. So many Aga owners use it as an extra shelf, rendering it completely useless for the job it is intended for. I really do recommend buying a second Cold Plain Shelf if you are a keen baker. It must be kept outside the Aga, not inside one of the ovens. The Cold Plain Shelf will give you a moderate oven for about 30-40 minutes. So if you are a 2-oven Aga owner, for cakes requiring more than 40 minutes use a Cake Baker. For 4-oven Aga owners, use the Baking Oven, although you will notice some recipes will start in the Roasting Oven. Plan your baking when the ovens are cooler, such as after you have had a big cooking session.

Tins are crucial when baking and the heavier the better. Loose-bottomed or spring form tins are so much easier to use. Weigh ingredients, preferably on a digital scale. I use large eggs, a set of specific kitchen measuring spoons, and a measuring jug for liquids. My most used bit of kit is my trusty Kitchen Aid Mixer.

As a general rule, when baking cakes I have found that the two best positions for baking are either with the grid shelf on the lowest set of runners in the Roasting Oven with the Cold Plain Shelf above on the second set of runners, or with the grid shelf on the floor of the Roasting Oven and the Cold Plain Shelf on either the third or fourth set of runners, depending how high the cake tin is. Most cakes take roughly 20 minutes to cook. Check the cake regularly while it is baking; opening the oven door will not impair cooking results – in fact I have cooked a Victoria Sponge with the oven door completely off and it was fine.

A word about fruit cakes

I have included my recipe on page 143 for a fruit cake that I make once a week in winter. I also use the recipe for my Christmas cake. I believe that, in general, people tend to stick to the same recipe, but it is the Aga method they want to know about more than a new recipe.

When it comes to baking your fruit cake, the best oven in the world is the 2-oven Aga Simmering Oven. Prepare your fruit cake recipe as usual and then place the tin on the third set of runners in the Simmering Oven. On average, a 20 cm round fruit cake will take anything from 4 to 10 hours. The reasons for the timing variation are that no two Aga cookers are the same and the newer ones have better insulation. My standard fruit cake recipe in the Simmering Oven takes about 6 hours.

Owners of a 4-oven Aga may find their Simmering Oven is slower than a 2-oven Aga Simmering Oven. The cake will probably cook better if started in the Baking Oven for 45-60 minutes, then transferred to the Simmering Oven in as high a position as possible and cooked for anywhere from 4-10 hours or even longer in some cases. Another trick is to use the large grill rack from the Large Roasting Tin. Put the grill rack directly onto the Simmering Oven Floor and put the cake tin on it for cooking. If you feel you don't need the extra boost of the Baking Oven, bake the cake in the Simmering Oven only as above.

Lining the tin with Bake-O-Glide is all the tin preparation you need. There's no need for brown paper or newspaper for lining and covering the cake. Another good method for cooking fruit cake is the Aga Cake Baker (see page 10). The only drawback is that you are restricted to the size and shape of the tins.

chocolate fruit cake

serves at least 12

175 g candied mixed lemon and orange peel, preferably organic, roughly chopped

70 g Griottines cherries

30 g dried sour cherries

60 g raisins

170 ml rum

15 g cherry jam

454 g jar runny honey

zest of 1 lemon

120 g whole hazelnuts

80 g blanched whole almonds

80 g unblanched whole almonds

80 g flaked almonds

120 g unsalted butter, softened

60 g golden caster sugar

120 g plain flour

3 large eggs

200 g ground almonds

300 g very best dark chocolate, roughly chopped

1 Line a 20 cm diameter cake tin with Bake-O-Glide. If you are using the cake baker method, heat the cake baker in the ROASTING OVEN whilst mixing the cake.

2 Put the candied peel, cherries, raisins, rum, cherry jam, honey and lemon zest in a bowl and marinate for 3 hours – the longer you marinate, the better.

3 Roast the hazelnuts and blanched almonds on the second set of runners in the ROASTING OVEN for 3-5 minutes or until brown. Peel and roughly chop all of the whole nuts.

4 Cream the butter and sugar, sift in the flour, then add the eggs one at a time. Add 120 g of the ground almonds and mix well.

5 Add the fruit and nuts to the butter and sugar mixture, along with the remaining ground almonds and the chocolate. Pour the mixture into the cake tin.

6 Put the cake tin into the Cake Baker and cook for approximately 1¾-2 hours on the floor of the ROASTING OVEN. If you are using the SIMMERING OVEN, put a grid shelf into the SIMMERING OVEN – the runners you use will depend how high the cake tin is. In general, aim for the fourth set of runners or on the floor. Put the tin on the grid shelf and cook for 4-8 hours or until the cake is cooked. Check the cake is cooked by inserting a skewer into the middle of the cake. If it comes out clean, the cake is done. Cool the cake in the tin. The cake can be frozen for 2 months or kept well wrapped in cling film and foil for up to a month.

Conventional Cooking:

Pre-heat the oven to 140°C/275°F/gas 1 and bake the cake for 4-4½ hours or until a skewer comes out clean.

sephardic orange cake

serves 8

2 oranges, preferably organic	225 g ground almonds
6 eggs	1 tsp baking powder
175 g caster sugar	

1 Place the oranges in a saucepan of water and heat to boiling point on the BOILING PLATE, then transfer the pan to the SIMMERING OVEN for 1 hour, then drain and process the oranges – skin and all – until puréed in a food processor.

2 Line a 20 cm round cake tin with deep sides with Bake-O-Glide. If you are using a Cake Baker, pre-heat it in the ROASTING OVEN while you mix together the cake ingredients.

3 Whisk the eggs and sugar until meringue-like in an electric mixer, then fold in the rest of the ingredients and mix well. Pour into a prepared cake tin and cook for 50-60 minutes in the Cake Baker on the floor of the ROASTING OVEN or in a regular cake tin on the fourth set of runners of the BAKING OVEN. Cool and serve with whipped cream and a citrus sorbet.

Conventional Cooking;
Pre-heat the oven to 190°C/375°F/gas 5 and bake as above in a cake tin.

apple cake

serves 8

260 ml sunflower oil	pinch of salt
30 ml hazelnut oil	1 tsp cinnamon
450 g caster sugar	1 tsp vanilla extract
700 g plain flour	3 large eggs
1 tsp baking soda	4 large cooking apples, peeled, cored and chopped into small cubes
2 tsp baking powder	

1 If you use the Cake Baker, put it in the ROASTING OVEN to preheat. Grease or line a 20 cm round cake tin with Bake-O-Glide.

2 Tip all the ingredients into a large mixing bowl and mix together really well.

3 Pour the mix into the prepared tin and bake in the Cake Baker on the ROASTING OVEN floor for 1¼ hours or until a skewer comes out clean. Owners of 4-oven Aga can use the BAKING OVEN and bake the cake for about 1 hour or until a skewer comes out clean. If it browns too quickly, slide in the COLD PLAIN SHELF above the cake.

4 Remove the cake from the oven and cool in the tin on a wire rack. When the cake is cool, remove from the tin. Serve with thick double cream.

Conventional Cooking:
Pre-heat oven to 190°/375°F/gas 5 and bake for about 1 hour.

right: sephardic orange cake

all-in-one victoria sponge cake

serves 6-8

175 g self raising flour
175 g soft unsalted butter
175 g caster sugar
1 tsp vanilla extract
3 large eggs
1 rounded tsp baking powder

FOR THE FILLING:

285 ml whipped cream
2 punnets soft fruits, such as blueberries, strawberries, loganberries
icing sugar, for dusting

1 Line two 20 cm round sponge tins, preferably loose bottomed, with Bake-O-Glide. Put all the cake ingredients into the bowl of an electric mixer and, using the beater attachment, beat until combined. Divide the cake mix between the prepared cake tins.

2 Place the grid shelf on the floor of the ROASTING OVEN and place the cake tins towards the right side of the oven, on the grid shelf. Slide the COLD PLAIN SHELF onto the third set of runners and bake the cakes for 20 minutes or until they are golden on top, gently coming away from the sides and spring back when lightly pressed on top. Remove the cakes and stand on a wire rack for a minute, then remove the cakes from the tins and cool on the wire rack. For 4-oven Aga owners, cook the cakes on the fourth set of runners in the BAKING OVEN for 20-25 minutes and use the plain shelf only if the cakes are browning too quickly.

3 When the cakes are cool, whip the cream to soft peaks and spread onto one cake then top with the fruits and the second cake. Dust with icing sugar and serve.

Conventional Cooking:

Pre-heat the oven to 160°C/325°F/gas 3 and bake for 30-35 minutes.

buttermilk scones

makes about 10 scones using a 6 cm cutter

475 g self-raising flour
50 g caster sugar
1 level tbsp baking powder
pinch of salt
355 g butter, softened

2 large eggs
120 ml buttermilk

FOR THE GLAZE:

1 egg yolk beaten with 1 tbsp milk

1 Line two baking trays with Bake-O-Glide.

2 Combine the flour, sugar, baking powder and salt in the bowl of an electric mixer with the paddle hook. Add the butter in pieces.

3 Lightly beat the eggs and the buttermilk together, then add them to the flour and butter. Mix until the dough just starts to hold together. Turn out onto a floured surface and knead for no more than 1 minute.

4 Roll out the dough about 2 cm thick and cut out the scones with a fluted 6 cm cutter. Put them onto the prepared baking trays and brush with the egg and milk glaze. Sprinkle over a little more sugar if you wish. Slide the baking tray onto the third set of runners in the ROASTING OVEN and bake for 8-10 minutes or until they are golden. Remove from the oven and cool on a wire rack.

Conventional Cooking:

Pre-heat the oven to 220°C/425°F/gas 7 and bake for 10-12 minutes until golden and well risen.

right: all-in-one Victoria sponge cake

gorgonzola scones

makes about 10 scones using a 6 cm cutter

475 g self raising flour
1 level tbsp baking powder
Pinch of salt
355 g butter, softened
2 large eggs
120 ml double cream

235 g Gorgonzola cheese, cut into small pieces and tossed in 1 tbsp self-raising flour

FOR THE GLAZE:
1 egg yolk beaten with 1 tbsp milk

1 Combine the flour, baking powder and salt in the bowl of an electric mixer with the paddle hook. Add the butter in pieces.

2 Lightly beat the eggs and the cream together and add them to the flour and butter. Add the Gorgonzola and mix until the dough just starts to hold together. Turn out onto a floured surface and knead for no more than 1 minute.

3 Roll the dough 2 cm thick and cut out scones with a fluted cutter. Line two baking trays with Bake-O-Glide. Put the scones on the prepared baking trays and brush with the egg glaze. Slide the baking tray onto the third set of runners in the ROASTING OVEN and bake for 8-10 minutes or until they are golden. Remove from the oven and cool on a wire rack.

Conventional Cooking:
Pre-heat the oven to 220°C/425°F/gas 7 and bake for 10-12 minutes until golden and well risen.

chocolate chip cookies

makes 25-30 cookies

500 g unsalted butter, softened
900 g soft unrefined brown sugar
235 g granulated sugar, unrefined
4 large eggs
1 vanilla pod with the seeds scraped out

1 kg plain flour
1½ tsp salt
2 tsp baking powder
500 g plain chocolate chips

1 Cream the butter and sugars in an electric mixer until smooth and fluffy. Add the eggs one at a time and scrape in the vanilla seeds.

2 Sift the flour, salt and baking powder into the butter mix. Fold to combine, then add the chocolate chips.

3 Line a large baking tray with Bake-O-Glide. Using a tablespoon, drop spoonfuls of the cookie dough onto the baking tray 4 cm apart.

4 Bake for 6 minutes on the second set of runners in the ROASTING OVEN. For 4-oven Aga owners, slide the cookies onto the third set of runners in the BAKING OVEN and cook for 6-8 minutes. The cookies should be golden on the outside but chewy in the middle. Cook in batches and cool on wire racks.

5 This dough freezes well. Spoon the raw dough into the middle of a large sheet of greaseproof paper and shape into a log. Roll the paper up and tie with string at the ends. Wrap in cling film and foil. To bake the cookies, simply cut slices off the frozen dough and put them on to a lined baking tray. Bake as above but for an extra 2 minutes.

Conventional Cooking:
Pre-heat the oven to 190°C/375°F/gas 5 and bake for 8 minutes.

chocolate brownies

makes about 10 brownies

300 g dark chocolate, chopped	1 shot of espresso or 1 tsp instant espresso powder
230 g butter	110 g plain flour
340 g caster sugar	2 tsp baking powder
3 large eggs	pinch of salt (if you use salted butter, omit this)
2 tsp vanilla extract	100 g chopped pecans or nuts or your choice

1 Melt the chocolate and butter either at the back of the Aga or in the SIMMERING OVEN. Set aside to cool for about 5 minutes. Grease a 24 x 34 cm, 3 cm deep baking tray.

2 Stir together the sugar, eggs, vanilla extract and espresso. Pour the egg mix into the chocolate and sift over the flour, baking powder and salt. Dust the chopped nuts with a teaspoon of flour (it stops them from sinking into the mix) and add. Give the mix a really good stir, then pour into the greased baking tray.

3 Bake on the third set of runners in the ROASTING OVEN for 15 minutes, then tap the side of the tin to release any air bubbles. Slide in the COLD PLAIN SHELF on the second set of runners and move the tin to the fourth set of runners. Continue baking for a further 15-20 minutes. If you have a BAKING OVEN, bake on the third set of runners for 20 minutes, then continue as above. Test with a skewer, it is done when it comes out clean. Don't overcook as you want the brownies to be slightly squidgy.

4 Cool thoroughly, then cut into squares and keep in an airtight tin or in the refrigerator. These brownies can be made 3 days in advance (if you can resist eating them for that long!).

Conventional Cooking:

Pre-heat the oven to 180°C/350°F/gas 4 and bake for 30-35 minutes.

shortbread biscuits

These are the biscuits we serve at my Aga demonstrations. Halve the quantities if you want to make less.

makes about 50 biscuits

900 g butter, at room temperature
450 g caster sugar
1.25 kg plain flour

225 g semolina
5-6 drops orange extract or other flavouring (optional)
extra caster sugar, for sprinkling

1 Cream together the butter and sugar until pale and fluffy in an electric mixer with the paddle attachment. Sift in the flour and semolina and add the orange extract if using.

2 Combine well, then scrape the mixture into the large roasting tin, cover with cling film and chill overnight.

3 The next day, cut the dough into 4 or 5 blocks and remove from tin. Cut each block into 2 cm thick squares and put onto a baking tray lined with Bake-O-Glide. Slide the tray onto the third set of runners in the BAKING OVEN for 20-25 minutes, or the fourth set of runners in the ROASTING OVEN with the COLD PLAIN SHELF on the second set of runners for 10-15 minutes, or until lightly coloured.

4 Remove the shortbread to a wire rack to cool and sprinkle with more caster sugar – this must be done while the biscuits are still hot.

5 The dough freezes well. If you want to use only a few blocks of dough, wrap the remaining blocks very well in cling film and foil and freeze until required. When you want to bake them, slice into the biscuit shapes and bake for 15-20 minutes from frozen as above.

Conventional Cooking;
Pre-heat the oven to 180°C/350°F/gas 4 and bake for 10 minutes.

focaccia bread

makes 1 loaf

30 g yeast	**FOR THE TOPPING:**
1 kg strong flour	1 tbsp rosemary, chopped
120 ml olive oil	1 tbsp thyme leaves
30 g salt	1 tbsp fennel top, chopped
	2 garlic cloves, peeled and sliced
	sea salt
	olive oil

1 Crumble the yeast into 200 ml warm water and mix until it is smooth.

2 Put the flour, olive oil and salt into the bowl of an electric mixer with the dough hook in place. Start the motor and slowly pour in the yeast and up to 350 ml warm water. You may or may not need all of the water so pour it in a little at a time. Knead until it becomes smooth and elastic. Don't be alarmed if it looks sloppy to begin with as it will pull together.

3 Lightly grease a large bowl and turn out the dough into it. Cover with a damp tea towel and place it next to the Aga for about an hour or until the dough has doubled in size.

4 While the dough is proving, mix together the herbs, garlic, salt and enough olive oil to slacken the mixture.

5 When the bread has had its first proving, knock it back by punching the air out. Line the large roasting tin with a large piece of Bake-O-Glide and shape the dough into the tin, stretching it to fit. Pour over the herb oil and, using your fingers, press the oil and herbs into the dough, giving it a dimpled effect. Leave the tin next to the Aga again for its second proving.

6 When the dough has doubled in size, place the tin on the floor of the ROASTING OVEN for 20-25 minutes. If it browns too quickly, insert the COLD PLAIN SHELF onto the third set of runners. Cool in the tin for a few minutes, then remove the bread from the tin and peel off the Bake-O-Glide. Transfer to a wire rack to finish cooling.

Conventional Cooking:
Pre-heat the oven to 220°C/425°F/gas 7 and bake for 30-40 minutes in the centre of the oven.

apricot and hazelnut bread

makes 2 large loaves

40 g fresh yeast	30 g salt
700 ml hand-hot water	100 g no-soak apricots, chopped
1 kg strong white flour	100 g hazelnuts, halved
250 g rye flour	

1 Mix the yeast into 200 ml of the water. Put a dough hook into an electric mixer (you can do this by hand but it will be hard work) and put the flours and salt into the bowl of the mixer. Turn the mixer onto a medium speed, then pour in the yeast and remaining water little by little. You may not need all of the water. When the dough starts to come together add the apricots and hazelnuts.

2 Knead for about 10 minutes on high, until it is smooth and pliable. Place the dough in a lightly oiled large bowl and cover with a clean, damp tea towel and put near the side of the Aga. Leave it to prove for 45-60 minutes or until it has doubled in size.

3 Knock back the dough by punching the air out and shape into loaf tins or into a round ball or long loaf on a piece of Bake-O-Glide on a baking sheet. Leave it for 35-40 minutes to prove a second time, then slide the tins or the Bake-O-Glide directly onto the floor of the ROASTING OVEN (discard the baking sheet) and bake for about 20-25 minutes. It is ready when the underside sounds hollow when tapped. Cool on a wire rack.

Conventional Cooking:
Pre-heat the oven to 220°C/425°F/gas 7 and bake for 30-40 minutes in the centre of the oven.

rye bread

makes 2 large loaves – eat one and freeze one!

40 g fresh yeast	250 g rye flour
700 ml hand-hot water	30 g salt
1 kg strong white flour	

1 Mix the yeast into 200 ml of hand-hot water. Put a dough hook into an electric mixer (you can do this by hand but it will be hard work) and put the flours and salt into the bowl of the mixer. Turn the mixer onto a medium speed, then pour in the yeast and water. Add a further 500 ml of hand-hot water a little at a time – you may or may not need all of the water – until the dough pulls away from the sides of the bowl.

2 Knead for about 10 minutes on high. The dough has been kneaded enough when it is smooth and pliable. Place the dough into a lightly oiled large bowl and cover with a clean damp tea towel and put near the side of the Aga. Leave it to prove for 45-60 minutes or until it has doubled in size.

3 Knock back the dough by punching the air out and shape into loaf tins or into a round ball or long loaf on a piece of Bake-O-Glide on a baking sheet. Leave it to prove in a warm place for a second time, for 30-45 minutes.

4 Slide the tins or the Bake-O-Glide directly onto the floor of the ROASTING OVEN (discard the baking sheet) and bake for about 20-25 minutes. It is ready when the underside sounds hollow when tapped. Let it cool on a wire rack.

Conventional Cooking:

Pre-heat the oven to 220°C/425°F/gas 7 and bake for 30-40 minutes in the centre of the oven.

refrigerator white bread

makes one loaf

1 kg strong white bread flour	30 ml sunflower oil, plus more for greasing
600 ml hand-hot water	25 g salt
25 g butter, softened	35 g fresh yeast

1 Put the dough hook into an electric mixer and add the flour, butter, oil and salt. Mix to combine.

2 Crumble the yeast into 425 ml of warm water, stir and when the yeast has melted, pour it into the flour. Add more warm water (to a maximum of 175 ml) if the dough is too stiff. It is best to hold back a little water and add if necessary rather than pour it all in and have to add more flour.

3 Knead for 8 minutes on a medium speed or until the dough is soft and elastic. Lightly oil a bowl and put the dough into the bowl. Cover with cling film and store in the fridge overnight.

4 When you are ready to bake the bread, remove the dough from the fridge and mould into shape on a piece of

Bake-O-Glide or in a tin. Let it rise near the Aga for 45-60 minutes or until it has risen.

5 Bake on the ROASTING OVEN floor for 20-25 minutes or until it sounds hollow when tapped on the underside. (If you are using Bake-O-Glide, put it onto a shallow baking tray and slide the paper off the tray and onto the floor of the oven.) Cool on a wire rack. The great thing about this dough is that you can pull off small amounts to bake and leave the rest in the fridge for up to 2 days.

Conventional Cooking:

Pre-heat the oven to 220°C/425°F/gas 7 and bake for 30-40 minutes in the centre of the oven.

pizza dough

makes dough for 2 medium-sized pizzas

40 g fresh yeast
175 ml hand-hot water
125 ml milk, at room temperature
300 g '00' flour

40 g strong plain flour
5 g salt
olive oil, for greasing bowl

1 Crumble the yeast into milk and 175 ml hand-hot water and leave for 10 minutes.

2 Mix the yeast with the sifted flours and knead for 10 minutes. The dough should be sticky. Add more flour if necessary. Whatever happens, do not end up with a stable dough! It should be threatening to stick to the sides of the bowl.

3 Cover the bowl with a damp tea towel. Let the dough rise in an oiled bowl next to the Aga for about 1 hour or until doubled in size.

4 Shape dough into a pizza shape – pull and stretch it but do not roll. You can freeze it at this point. When you want to use it, thaw and continue as below.

5 Shape the dough into the pizza circle directly onto a large piece of Bake-O-Glide. This makes it much easier to slide into the oven.

6 Let the dough rise for about 10 minutes, then add the toppings and bake. You can use the recipe for Balsamic Roasted Tomato Sauce on page 188 as a base sauce, then top with mozzarella cheese, pepperoni, Parma ham, black olives or anything you fancy. Cook the pizza directly on the floor of the ROASTING OVEN for 12-14 minutes.

Conventional Cooking:

Use a baking stone for best results. Pre-heat the stone in the oven at 220°C/425°F/gas 7 and cook the pizza directly on the stone in the oven. Follow the stone manufacturer's instructions.

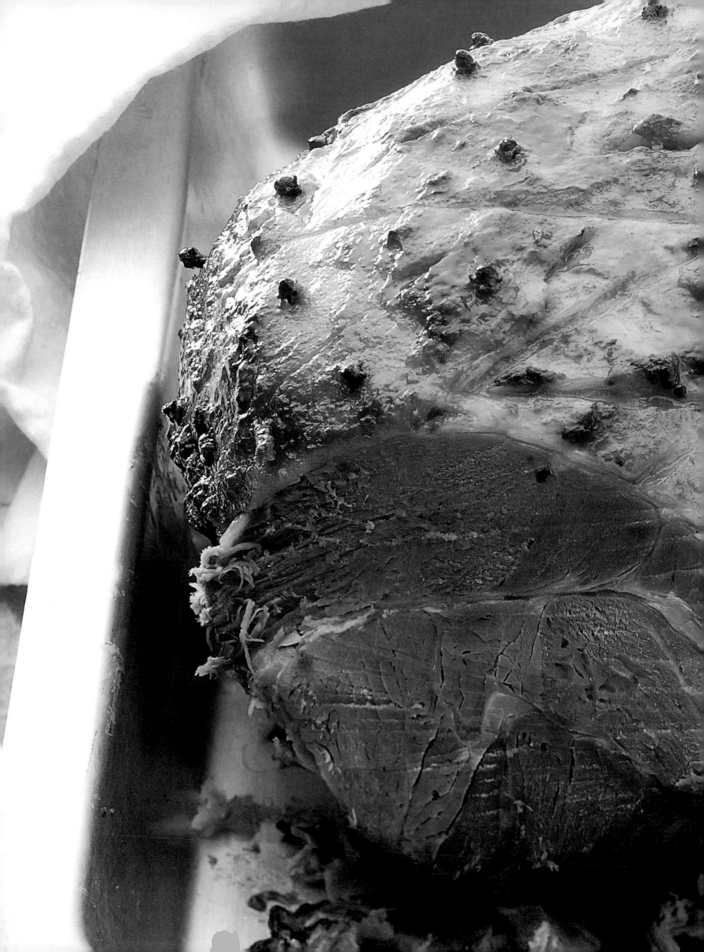

christmas
entertaining

Christmas Cooking Timetable

Christmas doesn't have to be a hectic rush with all preparation left to the last minute. With a large glass of wine, a deep breath and a little planning, this timetable will guide you through the Christmas holidays.

Early December:

Order fresh turkey. If you are buying a frozen turkey, do it now. It is best to allow 4-5 days for it to thaw so having it to hand will be an advantage. Make and freeze the mince pies.

One week before Christmas:

Start to defrost turkey at the back of the fridge. Write shopping lists and purchase all non-perishables. Buy milk in cartons and freeze in case of emergency.

Two days before Christmas:

Make cranberry sauce (see page 162) and store in the fridge. For stuffings and bread sauce you will need stale bread. Cut and cube it now and lay it out on a baking tray in a single layer.

Christmas Eve:

Morning:

Collect fresh turkey. Buy fresh fruit and vegetables. Prepare giblet gravy. Defrost mince pies.

Afternoon:

Prepare stuffings. Leave well covered in a cool place, but not in the refrigerator, as it shouldn't be too cold when you stuff the turkey.

Prepare vegetables. Peel potatoes and put in cold water in the fridge. Prepare other vegetables and store in polythene bags and refrigerate. Or start the 'get ahead vegetables' off – make the roast potatoes and blanche the other vegetables (see page 110).

Make bread sauce (see page 187) and store in the fridge, taking care to cover the surface with cling film.

Before you retire to bed:

Take turkey out of the fridge to allow it to come to room temperature. Do the same with the stuffing and butter so that it softens for the morning. If you are cooking a turkey using the overnight method (see page 63), calculate the timings and start cooking it. With all the newly created space, fill up the fridge with wines, minerals, etc.

Christmas Day

Aga owners are always worried about running out of heat so to prevent this, write out a preparation schedule and a cooking timetable. This timetable is based on a 7 kg turkey, to be served at 2pm.

7:30am
Stuff the turkey.

8:15am
Put the turkey in the oven and baste with melted butter every 30 minutes. If you are using the Warming Oven in a 4-oven Aga, put in the required plates and serving dishes.

11:30am
Prepare bacon rolls and chipolatas. Re-heat bread sauce and place it in a jug with butter on top to melt over the surface, keep warm.

12:00
Start steaming the Christmas pudding. Bring to the boil on the BOILING PLATE, then transfer to the SIMMERING OVEN for 3 hours.

12:45pm
If you are cooking your vegetables conventionally, do roast potatoes and prepare saucepans of boiling water for any other vegetables.

1:15pm
Remove turkey from oven, cover loosely with foil and let it rest. Make gravy (see page 162) and keep warm.

1:30pm
Check chipolatas and bacon rolls, remove and keep warm. Put in 'get ahead' roast potatoes.

1:45pm
Put sprouts on to cook or put in 'get ahead' blanched vegetables. While they are cooking, transfer the other food into serving dishes and carve the turkey. Check Christmas pudding.

2:00pm
Serve Christmas lunch.

pistachio and apricot stuffing

This can be made ahead and put into the fridge the day before. Bring to room temperature before cooking.

serves 12

2 tbsp olive oil
2 large onions, peeled and finely chopped
60 g pistachio nuts, chopped
60 g butter
120 g ready-to-eat dried apricots

175 g fresh white breadcrumbs
4 tbsp chopped flat-leaf parsley
zest of 1 lemon
1 egg, beaten

1 Heat the oil in a frying pan and sweat the onions until very soft on the ROASTING OVEN floor. Add the pistachio nuts and fry on the SIMMERING PLATE until golden.
2 Next, tip in the remaining ingredients and stir to combine. Shape into 12 balls and put into a buttered baking dish. Drizzle with a little more olive oil and bake on the third set of runners in the ROASTING OVEN for 30 minutes or until golden.

Conventional Cooking:
Pre-heat the oven to 180°C/350°F/gas 4 and cook for 45 minutes.

turkey

The stuffing for this recipe is made from the legs of the turkey.

serves 12-14

7 kg turkey (size depends on how many people you intend to serve; remove gizzard and use for stock)

2 medium onions, peeled and chopped

1 garlic clove, peeled and crushed

175 g vacuum-packed chestnuts, chopped

2 tbsp chopped sage, plus 6 sprigs whole sage leaves

2 eggs per 500 g of minced turkey meat

a good handful of herbs – sage, bay or other large leaf herbs left whole and in good condition

4 tbsp unsalted butter, for basting

salt and pepper

1 First, remove both legs and bone them (if possible, get your butcher to do this), making sure all the sinews are removed. Open out the boned legs and cut off about a quarter of the inside meat (the meat is mostly in flaps and is easy to cut away). Be very careful not to tear the skin. Mince the leg meat in a food processor, weigh and set aside.

2 Sweat the onions and garlic in a frying pan on the SIMMERING PLATE until soft. In a large bowl, combine the minced leg meat, onions, garlic, chestnuts, sage, salt and pepper and the eggs. Lay out the sage sprigs on a large piece of greased foil, then put the prepared legs skin side down on top. Divide the stuffing between the legs, then carefully roll up the legs, twisting the ends of the foil tightly. Set aside until ready to cook.

3 Gently loosen the breast skin away from the meat with your fingers, taking great care not to tear the skin. Lift the skin carefully and arrange the herb leaves underneath the skin in a pretty pattern. Refrigerate until ready to cook. All of the above can be done the day before.

4 When you are ready to cook the turkey, melt about 4 tablespoons of unsalted butter in a bowl and keep near the oven with a pastry brush so that you are ready to baste the breast.

5 Cook the legs and breast in the ROASTING OVEN, on the last set of runners or wherever the roasting tin fits, for about 1¾ hours, basting the breasts with butter every 15 minutes or so. Check the turkey breast after 1½ hours to see if it is cooked – insert a skewer and if the juices run clear it is done, if not put it back into the oven for another 15 minutes and check again. The legs will need the full 1¾ hours. Check to see if they are cooked by inserting the skewer. If at any point the breast skin starts to burn, cover with a piece of foil.

6 Let the cooked turkey rest for at least 20 minutes before carving. Make the gravy and serve with Cranberry and Walnut Sauce (see page 162).

Conventional Cooking:
See page 63 for conventional roasting times.

maple glazed turkey with orange and herb stuffing

serves 8-10

5.5 kg turkey

1 whole orange

1 onion, peeled

FOR THE GLAZE:

200 ml maple syrup

80 g Dijon mustard

50 g butter

2 tbsp Worcestershire sauce

FOR THE STUFFING:

1 day-old 'country-style' loaf, cut into cubes

4 heaped tbsp freshly chopped parsley

1 onion, peeled and chopped

zest of 3 oranges

1 tbsp fresh thyme leaves

65 g butter, softened

2 large eggs, lightly beaten

120 ml orange juice

80 ml water

salt and pepper

1 First make the stuffing. Tip all the ingredients into a large bowl and mix together really well. Add more orange juice if it is too dry – all breads are different and you will have to judge the moistness – the mixture should hold together without being too loose. Butter a large casserole and fill with the stuffing. Cover with foil and bake on the third set of runners in the ROASTING OVEN for 40-45 minutes or until cooked.

2 Cut the orange and onion in half. Season the inside of the turkey with salt and pepper. Push the orange and onion into the turkey. Mix the glaze ingredients together and set aside.

3 Cook the turkey according to your usual method (see page 63). I always baste my turkey with melted butter and cover it with foil for the first 3½ hours of cooking. For this size bird allow about 4-4½ hours. If you stuff the bird, it will probably take an extra hour. Only stuff the neck end of the bird.

4 Remove the foil and pour over the maple glaze 30 minutes before the end of the cooking time.

Conventional Cooking:

To cook the stuffing, pre-heat the oven to 190°C/375°F/gas 5 and bake for 45-50 minutes.

best ever gravy

This is my method for making gravy and I always make lots of it so that we don't run out. Although I subscribe to the view 'I'd rather have a little really excellent gravy than a lot of bad gravy', my children do not – they want lots of really excellent gravy! It doesn't matter what you are roasting, the method is still the same. I use onions as a rack for the meat to sit on while it is roasting.

1 Cut two onions in half and rest the joint on top. When the joint is ready, remove it from the tin and let it rest covered with foil for 15-20 minutes. Spoon off any excess fat, leaving about 1-2 tablespoons in the tin along with the onions.

2 While the meat is resting, put the tin directly onto the SIMMERING PLATE and bring the juices to a simmer. Add 1 tablespoon of flour to the fat, onions and meat juices and whisk it in. Keep whisking until the flour absorbs all of the fat, adding a little more flour if necessary.

3 Whisking constantly so that there are no lumps, pour in about 100 ml of wine and a tablespoon of redcurrant jelly or any other fruit jelly, such as apple jelly with pork and mint jelly with lamb. Still whisking, pour in about 500 ml of home-made stock or less for a thicker gravy or more for a thinner consistency. This is where the quality of the stock is paramount – if you use inferior stock you will end up with inferior gravy.

4 When all of the liquid has been added, bring the gravy to a rapid simmer and cook for about 5 minutes. Check for seasoning and add salt and pepper to taste. It is very important to cook out the wine and the flour. Strain the gravy into a warmed jug and keep hot at the back of the Aga or in the SIMMERING or WARMING OVEN.

cranberry and walnut sauce

This sauce will keep for two weeks. Serve with turkey.

makes about 600 ml

340 g fresh cranberries	235 ml water
300 g caster sugar	235 g walnuts, coarsely chopped
235 g redcurrant jelly	2 tbsp orange zest

1 Combine cranberries, sugar, redcurrant jelly and 235 ml water in a large saucepan and bring to a rapid boil on the BOILING PLATE.

2 Move to the SIMMERING PLATE and simmer for 2 minutes. Skim off the foam and remove from the heat.

3 Stir in walnuts and orange zest. Pour into sterilised jars and cool.

Conventional Cooking;
Make this on the hob over a medium heat.

pomegranate glaze for roast turkey

for a 5 kg turkey

4 pomegranates	60 ml brandy
4 tbsp pomegranate molasses	1 tbsp redcurrant jelly

1 Cut two of the pomegranates in half and hold them cut side down over a bowl. Hit the back of the fruit very hard with a wooden spoon so the pips shower into the bowl. Set them aside.

2 Use a lemon juicer to squeeze out the juice from the remaining pomegranates. Put the pomegranate juice, pomegranate molasses, brandy and redcurrant jelly into a saucepan and heat to the boil on the BOILING PLATE.

Reduce the liquid so that it coats the back of a spoon.

3 Use your usual method of cooking the turkey. When there is only approximately 15 minutes left of cooking time for the turkey, remove it from the oven and baste the whole bird with the pomegranate glaze. Roast for 5 minutes. Baste the bird again and roast for final 10 minutes. Do not allow the glaze to burn. Rest the turkey for at least 20 minutes and serve.

mozzarella fondue

This is really a hot dip that everyone will love as it involves tomato sauce, mozzarella and ciabatta bread.

serves 6

1 tbsp extra virgin olive oil	2 x 400 g tins chopped tomatoes
3 anchovies, very finely chopped	1 tsp sugar
1 bunch of fresh basil leaves, torn	1 large ball (about 450 g) fresh buffalo mozzarella (or 2 smaller balls)
1 tsp fresh oregano leaves	
1 tsp balsamic vinegar	salt and pepper
3 garlic cloves, peeled and crushed	focaccia or ciabatta bread, torn into chunks

1 First, make the tomato sauce. Put the olive oil into a large saucepan and heat up on the SIMMERING PLATE. Add the anchovies, basil, oregano, balsamic vinegar, garlic, tinned tomatoes and sugar. Season with salt and pepper and bring up to a gently simmer.

2 Cover with a lid and transfer to the SIMMERING OVEN for 20 minutes. After 20 minutes, remove the lid and cook for another 10-15 minutes or until it has reduced a little. Taste and adjust the seasoning.

3 Pour the tomato sauce into a shallow ovenproof dish. Place the mozzarella into the centre of the sauce and transfer the dish to the third set of runners in the ROASTING OVEN and bake for 15-20 minutes or until the cheese almost melts completely. Serve with the bread.

Conventional Cooking:
Make the sauce on the hob. Pre-heat the oven to 220°C/425°F/gas 7 and bake for 20-25 minutes.

glazed ham for a crowd

Cooking a whole ham on the bone does take a bit of time but nothing tastes better than your own glazed ham and it will keep for ages.

5.5-6 kg ham will feed about 20 people

For the best flavour, I suggest buying an organic ham on the bone. Soak the ham in cold water. Ask the supplier what they recommend, as the soaking time will depend on how much salt is used when curing it. I usually use a plastic bucket or washing-up bowl, depending how big the ham is. I also change the water halfway through the soaking time. The next thing to do is to cook the ham. There are two options, boil and bake or bake only. The choice is yours.

To boil and bake:

1 Remove the ham from the soaking water and place it in a pot big enough to hold the ham yet still able to fit into the SIMMERING OVEN. Cover the ham with fresh cold water and bring to the boil on the BOILING PLATE. Transfer it to the SIMMERING PLATE and simmer for 20-30 minutes.

2 Transfer the ham to the SIMMERING OVEN for about 5 hours for a 5.5-6 kg ham or 6-6½ hours for a 6.5-7.5 kg ham. It is done when the juices run clear when a skewer is put through the thickest part.

3 Remove the ham from the water, peel off the skin and score the fat. Put the ham into the large roasting tin and push 20-30 whole cloves into the fat. Mix together 3-4 tablespoons of English mustard and 3-4 tablespoons of brown sugar. Press the sugar and mustard into the fat.

4 Hang the tin on the fourth set of runners of the ROASTING OVEN and bake the ham for 20-30 minutes or until it is nicely coloured and glazed. Eat the ham either hot or cold.

6.5-7.5 kg ham will feed about 30 people

To bake:

1 Remove the ham from the soaking water and drain. Lay two long pieces of foil in the large roasting tin, one lengthways, one widthways, so that it forms a cross. You need enough foil to allow the ham to sit in a tent of foil. Bring the foil up around the ham, leaving enough room for air to circulate around the joint.

2 Hang the tin on the fourth set of runners in the ROASTING OVEN and bake for 20 minutes per 450 g (a 5.5 kg ham will take approximately 4 hours). The ham is done when the juices run clear when a skewer is inserted to the thickest part of the ham.

3 Thirty minutes before the end of the cooking time, remove the joint from the oven, pull back the foil and remove the skin – it will be very hot so protect your hands. Score the fat and push 20-30 whole cloves into the fat and mix together 3-4 tablespoons of English mustard and 3-4 tablespoons of brown sugar. Press the sugar and mustard into the fat.

4 Hang the tin on the fourth set of runners of the ROASTING OVEN and bake the ham for 30 minutes or until it is nicely coloured and glazed. Eat the ham either hot or cold.

Conventional Cooking:

Prepare the ham as above. To cook, pre-heat the oven to 180°C/350°F/gas 4 and cook the ham for 20 minutes per 450 g. Before the final 30 minutes of cooking, turn the heat up to its highest setting (at least 220°C/425°F/gas 7), remove the foil cover and continue as above.

sausage rolls with cream cheese pastry

serves 12

700 g good-quality sausages with lots of flavour,
removed from their skins
Dijon mustard

FOR THE EGG WASH:
1 egg yolk mixed with 1 tbsp milk

FOR THE PASTRY:
175 g cream cheese
235 g butter, at room temperature
475 g plain flour
¼ tsp salt

1 Put the cream cheese and butter into the bowl of an electric mixer with the paddle attachment and beat until the cheese and butter are combined. Remove the paddle and replace it with the dough hook. Add the flour and salt to the cheese and combine on a low speed until it just starts to come away from the sides of the bowl. Shape into a round ball, wrap in cling film and chill overnight.

2 Line a baking tray with Bake-O-Glide. Remove the pastry from the fridge and cut in half. Roll out each half of pastry into a long oblong shape and carefully lay one half of the rolled pastry on the tray. Spread some Dijon mustard along the centre of the pastry. Shape the sausage meat into a long sausage shape and lay it on top of the mustard.

3 Lay the other oblong of pastry on top of the sausage meat and press the edges together. Make a couple of knife slashes along the top for steam to escape and brush the top with an egg wash.

4 Slide the baking tray onto the fourth set of runners in the ROASTING OVEN and bake for 20-25 minutes or until the top is golden and the sausage meat is cooked. If it starts to brown too quickly, slide the COLD PLAIN SHELF onto the second set of runners. For 4-oven Aga owners, slide the tray onto the third set of runners in the BAKING OVEN and bake for 20-25 minutes or until the top is golden and the sausage meat is cooked.

5 Remove from the oven, cool for a few minutes and cut into pieces and serve hot.

Conventional Cooking:
Pre-heat the oven to 200°C/400°F/gas 6 and cook for 25-30 minutes.

mincemeat

To sterilise jars and lids, run them through the hottest wash cycle in a dishwasher.

makes 3 kg

235 g organic mixed candied peel	¼ tsp ground cloves
235 g sultanas	150 g dried cranberries
350 g raisins	150 g dried sour cherries
500 g apples, peeled and grated	80 g flaked almonds
235 g suet, shredded	zest and juice of 2 oranges, preferably organic
400 g brown sugar	zest and juice of 2 lemons, preferably organic
½ tsp cinnamon	35 ml brandy
½ tsp allspice	grated nutmeg (about ½ a whole nutmeg)
2 cm piece of fresh ginger, grated	

1 Tip everything into a large, scrupulously clean heatproof bowl or casserole. Stir well and then put it on the floor of the SIMMERING OVEN for about 2-2½ hours or until the suet has melted.
2 Stir well so that all the fruit and nuts are well coated. Cover the bowl with a clean tea towel and stand overnight in a cool place.
3 The next day, stir the mincemeat again and spoon into the jam jars. Seal the jars with the lids and store in a cool dark place. The mincemeat will keep for about 6-8 months.

Conventional Cooking:
Pre-heat the oven to 120°C/250°F/gas ½ and place the bowl of mincemeat in the oven for 2-3 hours or until the fat has melted. Continue as above.

bacon munchies

These are very good served with drinks, and children love them too.

thickly sliced maple cured bacon	brown sugar
Dijon mustard	

1 Line the large roasting tin with Bake-O-Glide and set the grill rack in the tin.
2 Spread each piece of bacon with mustard on both sides, then pour the brown sugar onto a plate and press the mustard-coated bacon into the sugar on both sides. Make sure each piece is well coated in the mustard and sugar.
3 Lay the bacon on the grill rack and slide the tin onto the first set of runners in the ROASTING OVEN and grill for 4-5 minutes on each side or until the sugar has caramelised. Don't allow the bacon to burn. If the first set of runners is too hot, move the grill rack down to the second set. Let the bacon cool for a few minutes and then serve.

Conventional Cooking:
Cook the bacon under a hot grill for 3-4 minutes on each side.

chocolate pecan pie

serves 8

80 g dark chocolate
45 g unsalted butter
160 g granulated sugar
235 ml corn syrup or light golden syrup
3 eggs

1 tsp vanilla extract
235 g pecans, chopped
25 cm tart tin lined with uncooked pastry (see page 134), chilled

1 Melt the chocolate and the butter together either in a bowl over simmering water or in a microwave or at the back of the Aga and set aside.

2 In a medium-sized saucepan, combine the sugar and syrup and bring to the boil on the BOILING PLATE. Move to the SIMMERING PLATE for 2 minutes, stirring constantly, then set aside to cool.

3 Beat the eggs in a large bowl, then stir in the melted chocolate-butter mixture and whisk in the sugar syrup mixture so that it is all thoroughly combined. Add the vanilla extract and stir in the pecans. Set aside until completely cool.

4 Pour the filling into the chilled pastry. Place the pie on the ROASTING OVEN floor and bake for 20 minutes. Then slide in the COLD PLAIN SHELF on the second set of runners and move the pie to the grid shelf on the fourth set of runners. Continue to bake for a further 20-25 minutes. Cool and serve at room temperature.

Conventional Cooking:
Pre-heat the oven to 200°C/400°F/gas 6. Bake the pie for 20 minutes, then lower the temperature to 180°C/350°F/gas 4 and continue to cook for about 20 minutes until the pastry is golden and the filling is set.

christmas pudding snow drift

Serves 6

400 g Christmas pudding, crumbled
50 ml brandy
1 litre vanilla ice cream, softened

1 lemon
4 egg whites
225 g caster sugar

1 Put the Christmas pudding in a bowl and pour over the brandy. Let it stand for 30-60 minutes.

2 Beat the Christmas pudding into the softened ice cream so that it is evenly distributed. Mould the mixture into a dome shape on a metal baking tray and re-freeze so that it is extremely hard.

3 Make sure your bowl and whisk are scrupulously clean by rubbing a lemon half over the whisk and the inside of the bowl. Put the egg whites into the bowl and start to whisk the egg whites on a medium speed, increasing the speed to high as you go. First the whites will bubble and turn frothy, then they will form into soft floppy peaks and finally they will stiffen up to the stiff peak stage. Add the sugar one spoonful at a time.

4 Take the ice cream out of the freezer and spread the meringue mix over it. Slide the tray on to the fourth set of runners in the ROASTING OVEN. Bake for 8-10 minutes or until the meringue is golden. Serve immediately.

Conventional Cooking:
Pre-heat the oven to 200°C/400°F/gas 6 and cook for 8-10 minutes. Serve directly from the oven.

right: chocolate pecan pie

mummy's
little helpers

Cooking chicken nuggets couldn't be easier with an Aga, but here are some tempting recipes to entice your children to the table. Let your children help as much as possible. The best way to learn how to cook is 'at mother's knee'.

tuna and crisp casserole

serves 4

30 g butter	FOR THE WHITE SAUCE:
1 small onion, peeled and finely chopped	20 g butter
100 g mushrooms, sliced	10 g plain flour
185 g tin tuna fish in olive oil	115 ml warm milk
25 g packet prawn cocktail crisps, crushed	salt and pepper
235 g peas, cooked	
60 g packet ready salted crisps	

1 Make the sauce first. Melt the butter in a small saucepan on the SIMMERING PLATE. Add the flour and stir with a wooden spoon until it turns into a glossy paste. Pour in the warm milk a little at a time, stirring all the time until all the milk is incorporated and you have a smooth, lump-free sauce. Season and simmer for 3-5 minutes, whisking occasionally, so the flour is cooked. Don't let the sauce burn or catch on the bottom. Cover the surface of the sauce with cling film so a skin doesn't form.

2 Melt the butter in a saucepan on the SIMMERING PLATE and cook the onions and mushrooms until they are soft and tender. Mix them with half of the white sauce.

3 Drain the tuna and add to the mushrooms and white sauce mixture, along with the crushed prawn cocktail crisps and the cooked peas. Gently mix together and spoon into an ovenproof casserole. Top with the ready salted crisps.

4 Cook on the third set of runners in the ROASTING OVEN for 20-25 minutes. If it is browning too quickly, slide in the COLD PLAIN SHELF.

Conventional Cooking:
Pre-heat the oven to 200°C/400°F/gas 6 and cook for 25 minutes.

aga-toasted cheese sandwiches

You can use almost any filling you want to make toasted sandwiches. Let your tastebuds be your guide!

Butter two slices of bread. Spread some chutney on the unbuttered side and top with ham and grated cheese. Put the other slice of bread on top, buttered side up, and lightly press together. Open the lid of the SIMMERING PLATE, put the round piece of Bake-O-Glide on and lift the sandwich onto the hot surface. Close the lid and cook for 2-3 minutes. Open the lid, flip the sandwich over and cook for 2-3 minutes more or until the cheese has melted and the bread is golden. Serve straight away with soup or a salad.

Conventional Cooking:
Use a frying pan over a medium high heat and cook as above.

aga-baked chicken strips

makes about 24

450 g chicken breasts, skinned, boned and
cut into strips
235 ml buttermilk
160 g flour
½ tsp sweet paprika

475 g dry white breadcrumbs
3 large eggs
115 g butter, melted
salt and pepper

1 Line a baking tray with Bake-O-Glide and set aside. Put the chicken strips into a bowl and cover with the buttermilk. Leave to marinate for 30 minutes.

2 Combine the flour, paprika, salt and pepper on a flat plate. Beat the eggs in a shallow bowl. Spread out the breadcrumbs on another plate.

3 When the chicken is ready, dip each strip into the flour, then the eggs, and finally the breadcrumbs and lay out on the baking tray. Brush both sides of the chicken strips with the melted butter (at this point the chicken may be wrapped and frozen for up to 1 month).

4 Bake on the third set of runners in the ROASTING OVEN for 8-10 minutes or until they are crispy and golden brown. (If cooking from frozen, bake for 12-15 minutes.) Serve with ketchup.

Conventional Cooking:

Pre-heat the oven to 200°C/400°F/gas 6 and cook the chicken strips for 15 minutes or until golden and crispy. If cooking from frozen, cook for 20-25 minutes.

cheese and rice soufflé

serves 4

2 tbsp butter, plus more for greasing
3 tbsp flour
100 ml milk
4 egg yolks
225 g Cheddar cheese, grated

pinch of cayenne pepper
pinch of salt
50 g cooked rice
4 egg whites stiffly beaten

1 Grease a large soufflé dish with butter.

2 Make a roux by melting the butter in a small saucepan on the SIMMERING PLATE, then add the flour and stir well. Add the milk slowly, whisking until smooth. Next add the egg yolks and cheese and stir until the cheese has melted. Stir in the cayenne pepper, salt and rice. Mix well and remove from the heat.

3 Fold in the egg whites very gently, then pour into the soufflé dish. Place the dish on the baking tray.

4 With the grid shelf on the floor of the ROASTING OVEN and the COLD PLAIN SHELF on the second set of runners, place dish on the grid shelf and cook for 30-35 minutes until well risen and golden on top. Serve immediately.

Conventional Cooking:

Pre-heat the oven to 200°C/400°F/gas 6 and cook for 30-35 minutes.

pigs in blankets

makes 10 little piggies!

10 cooked frankfurters

FOR THE 'BLANKET' PASTRY:
475 g self-raising flour
1 level tbsp baking powder
pinch of salt

355 g butter, cubed and softened
2 large eggs
120 ml buttermilk

FOR THE GLAZE:
1 egg yolk beaten with 1 tbsp milk

1 Combine the flour, baking powder and salt in the bowl of an electric mixer with the paddle hook. Add the butter. Lightly beat the eggs and the buttermilk together, then add them to the flour and butter. Mix until the dough just starts to hold together.

2 Turn out onto a floured surface and knead for no more than 1 minute. Roll out the dough into a square shape 1 cm thick and cut into 10 oblong shapes, 10 x 8 cm. Wrap each piece of pastry around a frankfurter so the ends of the frankfurter peek out of the pastry 'blanket'.

3 Line two baking trays with Bake-0-Glide. Place the frankfurters on the baking trays and brush with the egg glaze. Slide the baking tray onto the third set of runners in the ROASTING OVEN and bake for 8-10 minutes or until they are golden. Remove from the oven and cool slightly on a wire rack. Serve with tomato ketchup.

Conventional Cooking:
Pre-heat the oven to 200°C/400°F/gas 6 and cook the pigs for 10-15 minutes until they are lightly golden.

mad hatter meatballs

serves 4

FOR THE SAUCE:
15 g butter
1 tbsp olive oil
1 small onion, peeled and minced
1 green pepper, finely chopped
1 clove garlic
400 g tin chopped tomatoes

FOR THE MEATBALLS:
1 egg, beaten
450 g minced beef
60 ml evaporated milk
2 slices of bread, whizzed up in a food processor to make fresh breadcrumbs
½ tbsp Worcestershire sauce
salt and pepper

1 First make the sauce. Melt the butter and the oil in a medium-sized ovenproof casserole dish on the SIMMERING PLATE. Cook the onion and green pepper until tender. Add the garlic and tomatoes, and season with salt and pepper. Bring to the boil, then simmer gently while you make the meatballs.

2 To make the meatballs, mix all the ingredients in a bowl, then use your hands to shape into balls about the size of ping-pong balls. Drop the meatballs into the simmering tomato sauce.

3 Transfer the casserole to the SIMMERING OVEN floor for 1-1½ hours or until the sauce has thickened and the meatballs are cooked. Serve with mashed potatoes.

Conventional Cooking:
Cook entirely on the hob and simmer for 45-60 minutes.

right: pigs in blankets

school fete cake

makes 20-24

70 g dark chocolate, chopped into pieces
250 g unsalted butter, diced
5 eggs
225 g caster sugar
275 g self-raising flour
3 tsp baking powder
3 tbsp double cream

FOR THE ICING:
200 g cooking chocolate
50 g unsalted butter
150 ml double cream

1 Put the chocolate and butter into a bowl and melt at the back of the Aga.

2 Line the large roasting tin with a sheet of Bake-O-Glide and set aside.

3 When the chocolate and butter have melted, pour it and the rest of the ingredients into the bowl of an electric mixer and mix well with the paddle attachment (you can do this with a hand whisk or electric hand whisk). Pour the cake mix into the prepared tin.

4 Hang the tin on the fourth set of runners of the ROASTING OVEN. Slide the COLD PLAIN SHELF onto the second set of runners and bake for 25–30 minutes or until it has risen, springs back when lightly pressed and is shrinking away from the sides of the tin. For 4-oven Aga owners, hang the tin on the fourth set of runners in the BAKING OVEN and bake for 30 minutes. Cool on a wire rack.

5 To make the icing, melt the chocolate and butter at the back of the Aga and stir well. Allow it to cool for a little while. Add the cream and mix until smooth and glossy. Cool for a few minutes, then pour over the cake and smooth with a knife. Cut into 20-24 squares.

Conventional Cooking:
Pre-heat the oven to 200°C/400°F/gas 6 and bake for 20-25 minutes.

magic bars

So delicious they disappear like magic!

makes 18

120 g unsalted butter
300 g digestive biscuit crumbs
375 ml can condensed milk

100 g dark chocolate chips
250 g desiccated coconut
200 g chopped pecans

1 Melt the butter in a shallow baking tin in the ROASTING OVEN for 1–2 minutes. Sprinkle the biscuit crumbs over the butter, pour the condensed milk evenly over the crumbs, then top with the remaining ingredients and press down.

2 Bake on the third set of runners in the ROASTING OVEN for 25-30 minutes or until golden in colour. If it is browning too quickly, slide in the COLD PLAIN SHELF. Cool on a wire rack, cut into squares and store at room temperature.

Conventional Cooking:
Pre-heat the oven to 180°C/350°F/gas 4 and bake as above.

vanilla fudge

makes 20-30 squares

300 ml whole milk
800 g caster sugar
100 g unsalted butter, plus extra for greasing

2 tsp vanilla extract
seeds of 1 vanilla pod

1 Bring the milk to the boil in a heavy-bottomed saucepan on the BOILING PLATE, then add the sugar and butter, stirring constantly until the sugar has dissolved and the butter melts.

2 Bring to the boil, cover with a lid and boil for 2 minutes. Uncover and continue to boil for 10-12 minutes or until it reaches the softball stage. You will be able to tell when it is at this stage by dropping a little of the mixture into ice-cold water. If it forms a softball it is ready, if not, continue to boil until this is achieved.

3 Remove the saucepan from the heat and stir in the vanilla extract and the vanilla seeds. Leave to cool for 5 minutes.

4 Butter a 24 x 35 cm Swiss roll tin. Beat the fudge well until it thickens, then pour into the buttered tin. Leave to cool. Mark into squares and cut with a knife when firm. Store in an airtight tin.

Conventional Cooking:
Cook on the hob over a medium heat.

cupcakes

makes 12 large cupcakes

275 g self-raising flour
200 g caster sugar
2 tsp baking powder
225 g unsalted butter or margarine
4 large eggs
4 tbsp milk

FOR THE BUTTERCREAM ICING:
3 large egg whites
155 g caster sugar
375 g unsalted butter, at room temperature
1 tsp vanilla extract

1 Line a muffin tin with paper cupcake cases and set aside.

2 Tip all the ingredients into a bowl and mix well until combined. Fill the cupcake cases to the top.

3 Bake on the fourth set of runners in the ROASTING OVEN for 20 minutes, checking halfway through and sliding in the COLD PLAIN SHELF if necessary. They are done when they spring back when gently pressed on top. Remove from the tin and cool on a wire rack. For 4-oven Aga owners, bake on the third set of runners in the BAKING OVEN for 20-25 minutes.

4 To make the icing, place the egg whites and sugar in a large heatproof bowl, over a pot of simmering water on the SIMMERING PLATE, and, using an electric whisk, whisk until the sugar has dissolved. When ready, take the bowl off the heat and continue whisking until it starts to form soft peaks. Add the butter bit by bit until it is all combined. Add the vanilla extract and chill until it becomes stiff but still spreadable, then use to ice the cup cakes. Add colouring if you wish.

Conventional Cooking:
Pre-heat the oven to 200°C/400°F/gas 6 and bake for 20-25 minutes.

on the side

aga preserving

There are a few golden rules when making jams, jellies and marmalades. Make them when your Aga is at its hottest, such as first thing in the morning. Always use dry, unblemished fruit. All equipment must be scrupulously clean. Jars and lids must be sterilized. If you have a dishwasher, put them through a high heat cycle, then place on a baking tray and put in the SIMMERING OVEN for 10-15 minutes. Keep them warm when you pour in the jam. Seal jars when hot.

Warm sugar and fruits in the SIMMERING or WARMING OVEN before using. If a recipe calls for a fruit that needs to be cooked before adding the sugar, do it in the SIMMERING OVEN. Use as little water as possible and cover the fruit with a tightly fitting lid. Bring to the boil on the BOILING PLATE, then transfer to the SIMMERING OVEN until it is ready.

Skim the scum off frequently when the jam is boiling or add a small knob of butter to disperse it.

To test for a good set, put a few saucers into a freezer before you start to cook the jam. After the first 20 minutes or so of rapid boiling, take a saucer out of the freezer and drop a small spoonful of the jam onto the cold saucer. Allow it to cool for a minute, then push your finger through the jam. If it wrinkles, it is ready; if not, boil the jam for a few minutes more. Carry on testing until a set has been reached. Always remove the jam from the heat when you are testing so that if it is ready you will not overcook the jam.

infused oils

lemon oil

1 organic lemon
4 stalks lemongrass

1 litre grapeseed oil
100 ml good-quality olive oil

1 Cut the peel away from the lemon. Bruise the lemongrass by bashing it with a rolling pin. Put the peel and lemongrass into a saucepan. Pour over the oils. Bring to the boil on the BOILING PLATE, then transfer to the SIMMERING OVEN for 30 minutes.
2 Remove from the oven and cover with cling film. Stand at room temperature overnight. Strain into a container,

adding one of the stalks of lemongrass to the container, and store. Use for garnishing salads, in salad dressings and fish dishes. The oil will keep for one month in the fridge.

Conventional Cooking:
Start off on the hob, then transfer to an oven pre-heated to 120°C/250°F/gas ½ for 30 minutes.

chilli oil

10 dried chillies
500 ml grapeseed oil

500 ml olive oil

1 Crush the dried chillies and put them into a saucepan. Pour over the two oils and bring to a simmer on the SIMMERING PLATE.
2 Take the saucepan off the heat and leave the oil to infuse for 5-7 days. Strain into a bottle and store. Use poured over pizzas, in salad dressings or when cooking spicy dishes.

Conventional Cooking:
Heat the oil in a saucepan on the hob.

lobster oil

4 lobster shells

grapeseed oil

1 Put the lobster shells in a heatproof dish, then pour over enough grapeseed oil and 2 tablespoons of water to cover the shells. Let the oil and the shells come to the boil on the BOILING PLATE, then transfer to the SIMMERING OVEN for 30 minutes.
2 Take out of the oven and stand at room temperature overnight. Strain into a jar and store for up to one month in the fridge. Use to garnish lobster salad or any fish dish.

Conventional Cooking:
Start off on the hob, then transfer to an oven pre-heated to 120°C/250°F/gas ½ for 30 minutes.

prune and apple chutney

makes about 4 x 500 g jars

15 g butter
1 tbsp sunflower oil
6 red onions, peeled and sliced
6 Granny Smith apples, peeled, cored and cut into small chunks
300 g brown sugar

250 g pitted prunes, cut into pieces
200 ml cider vinegar
zest and juice of 1 orange
1 tsp allspice
pepper

1 Melt the butter and oil in a large saucepan on the SIMMERING PLATE, add the onions and cook until they are soft.
2 Add the remaining ingredients and heat slowly on the SIMMERING PLATE until the sugar dissolves. Transfer to the BOILING PLATE and boil for 3-4 minutes, then move to the SIMMERING OVEN for 2-3 hours or until it is very thick and a spoon leaves behind a clean trail.

3 Ladle into sterilised jars, seal and label. Keeps for up to 6 months. Chutneys should be left to age for a minimum of 1 month before using.

Conventional Cooking:
Cook over a medium heat, then turn down the heat and gently simmer for 20-30 minutes or until the chutney is thick, as above.

seville orange marmalade

As a general rule, think in terms of 500 g sugar to each 500 ml of fruit pulp or juice instead of 1 lb of sugar to each pint.

makes 4 x 500 g jars

1.85 kg preserving sugar **1 lemon**
900 g Seville oranges **2.2 litres water**

1 Put the sugar at the back of the Aga to warm.

2 Cut the peel away from the oranges and chop up to the desired thickness and size. Place the peel in a pan and cover with 1.1 litres of water. Bring to the boil on the BOILING PLATE, then place in the SIMMERING OVEN for about an hour or until they are soft and tender.

3 While the peels are softening, cut the orange flesh up and put it and all the pips into a preserving pan with the remaining 1.1 litres of water and bring to the boil on the BOILING PLATE. Boil for 10 minutes. Transfer to the ROASTING OVEN for about 1 hour.

4 Remove the preserving pan from the ROASTING OVEN and strain the liquid through a large sieve with a bowl underneath to catch every last drop. Push the pulp with a wooden spoon so that you squeeze out as much pectin-rich liquid as possible.

5 Pour the liquid back into the preserving pan and add the sugar, zest and juice of 1 lemon to the liquid. Bring to the boil on the BOILING PLATE and then test for a set. To reach setting point it can take 15-20 minutes. When a set is reached, pour the marmalade into sterilised jars, seal and label.

Conventional Cooking:

Make in the usual way on top of the stove. Bring the orange peel to the boil and simmer over a medium heat for 30-35 minutes. Continue as above on top of the hob.

strawberry jam

makes 4 x 400 g jars

1 kg jam sugar **2 kg strawberries**

1 Put the sugar into a preserving pan or large heavy-bottomed saucepan (not cast iron), and place in the SIMMERING OVEN.

2 Hull and pick through the strawberries, discarding any blemished fruit. Put the fruit in the preserving pan and move the pan to the SIMMERING PLATE. Stir constantly until all the sugar has dissolved and the fruit releases its juices.

3 Move to the BOILING PLATE and boil rapidly for 4-5 minutes. Skim off any scum as it appears. Test for a set then, using a jam funnel, spoon into the prepared jam jars. Seal tightly with a screw-top lid while it is boiling hot and label.

Conventional Cooking:

Cook in the usual way on top of the hob.

right: Seville orange marmalade

apple, sage and mint jelly

You will need a jelly bag and somewhere to hang it while it drips. The upturned legs of a stool work well or buy a jelly bag stand.

adjust the quantities to suit

cooking apples – use as many as you have
water and/or apple juice to just cover the apples
cider vinegar – 145 ml to every 1 litre cooking liquor
sugar – 450 g to every 570 ml liquid

1 heaped tbsp chopped sage leaves to every 570 ml liquid

1 heaped tbsp chopped mint leaves to every 570 ml liquid

1 Wash the apples and cut them into chunks; do not peel or core them. Put them into a large pan and cover with water or apple juice if using so that the apple pieces are just covered.

2 Bring to the boil on the BOILING PLATE, then transfer to the SIMMERING OVEN for 45-60 minutes or until the apples are very pulpy.

3 Remove from the oven, add the vinegar and boil rapidly on the BOILING PLATE for about 5 minutes. Pour some boiling water through the jelly bag, then tip in the apple pulp. Hang the bag over a large bowl to catch all of the juice. Leave for a few hours or until all the juice has strained through. If you want a clear jelly do not squeeze the bag.

4 Measure the amount of liquid in the bowl and calculate the sugar amount required. Add 450 g sugar to every 570 ml of juice.

5 Put the sugar and apple juice back into the preserving pan or large pan and gently dissolve the sugar on the SIMMERING PLATE. When the sugar has completely dissolved, move to the BOILING PLATE and boil rapidly for 10-12 minutes. Test for a set. When you reach setting point, stir in the sage and mint. Ladle into sterilised jars, seal and label.

Conventional Cooking:
Make the jelly on the hob in the usual way.

red onion confit

makes 400 g

6 red onions	**1 tsp caster sugar**
2 tbsp olive oil	**1 tsp mixed spices**
1 tbsp butter	**salt and pepper**

1 Peel and slice the onions thinly. Put the oil and butter into a saucepan, add the onions and cook very gently on the SIMMERING PLATE until the butter has melted.

2 Add the sugar, spices, salt and pepper and stir well. Transfer the pan to the SIMMERING OVEN and cook for about 45 minutes or until the onions are soft and golden.

3 Spoon into a sterilised jar and cool. Store in the fridge for up to a week. Serve with pâté and cold meats.

Conventional Cooking:
Cook the onions over a medium heat on the hob, then simmer over a low heat until the onions are thick and soft.

right: apple, sage and mint jelly

white sauce

The sauce can be made in advance and gently re-heated. It is so useful as it is the base for many other sauces. Add cheese for a cheese sauce, onions softened in butter for an onion sauce, and almost any herbs can be used to make the sauce of your choice. If you are making béchamel sauce, infuse the milk with a chopped onion, parsley stalks and a blade of mace for about 10 minutes. Strain the milk and follow the recipe below.

makes 425 ml

40 g butter
20 g plain flour

425 ml milk, warmed
salt and pepper

1 Melt the butter in a small saucepan on the SIMMERING PLATE. Add the flour to the butter and stir well with a wooden spoon until it turns into a glossy paste.
2 Gradually pour in the warm milk, a little at a time, stirring or whisking all the time until all of the milk is incorporated and you have a smooth, lump-free sauce.
3 Simmer the sauce on the SIMMERING PLATE for

3-5 minutes, whisking occasionally, so that the flour is cooked. Do not let the sauce burn or catch on the bottom. Cover the surface of the sauce with cling film so a skin doesn't form.

Conventional Cooking:
Make in the usual way on the hob.

hollandaise sauce

For a mousseline of Hollandaise, fold in some whipped cream to the sauce before serving. For a Maltaise sauce, reduce the juice of one orange together with the zest by half and add this to the basic hollandaise recipe and serve. Alternatively, add 3 tablespoons of orange juice and ½ teaspoon of zest to the finished hollandaise sauce.

makes 350 ml

2 large egg yolks
juice of ½ a lemon
pinch of sugar

250 g unsalted butter, cut into cubes
salt and white pepper

1 Place the egg yolks, lemon juice, sugar, salt and pepper in a bowl with 1 tablespoon of water over a pan of simmering water (do not let the bowl come into contact with the water) and whisk until the mix leaves a ribbon trail.
2 Whisking constantly, drop in the cubes of butter one at a time. Don't drop in the next cube until the previous one

has been absorbed. This will take some time. When all the butter is used and you have a thick velvety sauce, taste for seasoning and serve.

Conventional Cooking:
Cook as usual on the hob.

bread sauce

serves 6-8

500 ml milk
6 whole cloves
1 medium onion, peeled and finely chopped
150 g stale white breadcrumbs or more if needed

30 ml thick double cream or crème fraîche
40 g butter
salt and pepper

1 Put the milk, cloves, chopped onion, salt and pepper into a saucepan and simmer on the SIMMERING PLATE for 15-20 minutes or until the onion is soft. Alternatively, bring to the boil on the BOILING PLATE and transfer to the SIMMERING OVEN for 20-30 minutes. Then take it off the heat and let it infuse for an hour or longer.

2 Just before serving, remove the cloves and sprinkle in the breadcrumbs. The breadcrumbs will swell after a while, but as you don't want a sauce that is too thick, don't be too quick to add more breadcrumbs. Stir in the cream and butter and pour into a warmed bowl. Serve with game, turkey and chicken.

Conventional Cooking:
Make the sauce on the hob. Infuse the milk off the heat and continue as above.

crème anglaise

To make lavender Crème Anglaise, omit the vanilla and infuse the milk with 2 sprigs of lavender that have been soaked in water for 4-6 hours in the fridge. If you can find lavender extract, add a few drops at the end of the recipe instead.

serves 4-6

2 egg yolks
½ tsp cornflour
300 ml milk

1 whole vanilla pod, split
2 tbsp caster sugar, or to taste

1 Whisk together the egg yolks and cornflour in a bowl, then set aside.

2 Pour the milk into a pan and scrape the vanilla pod seeds into the milk and add the sugar. Gently bring to a simmer on the SIMMERING PLATE. Take the milk off the heat and add to the egg yolks little by little, whisking constantly until they are all in.

3 Tip the mixture back into the saucepan. Place it on the SIMMERING PLATE and stir until it just coats the back of a wooden spoon. Serve the sauce either hot or cold.

Conventional Cooking:
Cook as usual on the hob.

balsamic roasted tomato sauce

serves 4

500 g vine tomatoes	1 bunch basil leaves
3 tbsp olive oil	100 g mascarpone cheese
1 tbsp balsamic vinegar	salt and pepper
1 tsp sugar	

1 Put the tomatoes in a deep-sided saucepan. Whisk the olive oil, balsamic vinegar, sugar, salt and pepper together and pour over the tomatoes. Stir in half the basil leaves.

2 Place the pan on the third set of runners in the ROASTING OVEN for 20-25 minutes or until the tomatoes are well cooked and very soft.

3 When they are ready, pour the tomatoes through a sieve over a small saucepan and then add the remaining basil leaves and the mascarpone cheese. Stir the cheese until melted, check seasoning and serve with spaghetti.

Conventional Cooking:
Cook the sauce on the hob over a medium heat, then simmer for 20 minutes and continue as above.

aga dried tomatoes

Remove any stalks from tomatoes, cut in half, remove the seeds and lay them cut side up on a piece of Bake-O-Glide on a baking sheet. Drizzle over some olive oil, a little salt and pepper and a sprinkling of caster sugar if desired. Place in the SIMMERING OVEN for 5-6 hours. Keep checking them and do not let them brown. When the tomatoes are firm and dry, take them out and leave to cool. Sterilise a jar and put the cooled tomatoes in with basil, chopped garlic, thyme or any other herb you fancy, cover with good olive oil and seal. Keep in the fridge.

aga baked breadcrumbs

To dry out breadcrumbs, sprinkle them onto a baking tray and slide them into the SIMMERING OVEN for 10 minutes, then, protecting the SIMMERING PLATE lid with a tea towel, set the tray on top and leave there until they are dry. For 4-oven Aga owners, slide the tray into the WARMING OVEN and leave until the breadcrumbs are dry.

yorkshire pudding

The jury is still out about whether one should or shouldn't let the batter stand for a few hours. To get ahead I make my batter the day before; if I'm pushed for time it stands for as long as it takes the fat to get up to temperature – the choice is yours.

serves 4

3 eggs	**salt and pepper**
175 g plain flour	**60 g dripping**
175 ml milk	

1 Whisk the eggs, then sift in the flour and whisk. Slowly add the milk and 110 ml water, whisking continuously. Season with salt and pepper. Set aside.

2 Put the dripping into the half-size roasting tin and heat it up in the ROASTING OVEN until it is smoking hot. Move the tin to the SIMMERING PLATE and pour in the batter. Hang the tin on the third set of runners in the ROASTING OVEN and cook for 25-30 minutes or until it has risen and is golden brown. Serve either straight away or cook it earlier in the day and re-heat for 8 minutes in the ROASTING OVEN before serving.

Conventional Cooking:

The reason Yorkshire puddings made in the Aga are so good is due to the high heat. Pre-heat the oven to its highest temperature and cook as above.

aga baked beans

serves 8-10

300 g navy beans, soaked in water overnight, then rinsed	**1 onion**
1 tomato, halved	**850 ml barbecue sauce**
1 hot chilli	**60 g brown sugar**
1 head of garlic, cut in half horizontally	**salt**

1 Put the beans, tomato, chilli, garlic and onion into a large casserole and cover with cold water. Bring to the boil on the BOILING PLATE for 10 minutes, then transfer to the SIMMERING OVEN for 35 minutes.

2 Discard the vegetables and strain the beans, reserving the cooking liquid. Pour the beans, cooking liquid, brown sugar and barbecue sauce into the casserole, cover and bring to the boil on the BOILING PLATE, then put back into the SIMMERING OVEN for 3½ hours or until most of the liquid has been absorbed. (It may be necessary to cover only slightly with a lid.)

Conventional Cooking:

Start the recipe off on the hob over a medium heat, then transfer the beans to an oven pre-heated to 150°C/300°F/gas 2 and cook for 3 hours.

index

soft fruit soufflé 133
frying 19, 96
fudge, vanilla 177

garlic
    roasted 122, 123
            butter 125
            and onion soup 35
    rouille 38, 39
gravy, best ever 162
grilling 11, 19
grouse, roast 62

ham
    flat bread with Parma ham 40
    glazed ham for a crowd 164-5
heat loss 9, 10, 18
herring, devilled roes on toast 48
hollandaise sauce 26, 186

'ironing' on the Aga 16

jar opening on the Aga 16

kettles 10, 14
kippers 23

lamb
    braised with prunes and
        apricots 52
    gigot boulangère 82
    grilled chump chops 81
    herb crusted loin of 81
    Persian slow-roasted shoulder
        92-3
    roasting 80
    shepherd's pie 91
leeks vinaigrette 37
lemon
    oil 180
    pudding 132
    verbena baked custard 132
lentils with pinenuts, lemon and
    mint 120
lobster oil 181

magic bars 176

marmalade, Seville orange 182,
    183
meat
    cooking methods 19, 80
    see also beef; lamb; pork
meatloaf, old-fashioned 48
meringues 129
mincemeat 167
mozzarella fondue 163
muffins 14, 19, 24
mushrooms 22
    stir-fried 116

noodles, stir-fried chicken with
    54-5

oils, infused 180-2
onions, red onion confit 184
oranges
    orange and herb stuffing 161
    sephardic orange cake 144,
        145
    Seville orange marmalade 182,
        183
ovens 8-9, 10-12, 18
    cleaning 14-15

panattone pudding 130-1
pancakes 28
pancetta and chestnut soup 33
parsnips, baked with apples 120
partridge
    roast 62
        with foie gras and figs 71
passionfruit, glazed tart 134, 135
pasta, cooking 19, 46
pastry, sweet 134
pheasant
    with cider 65
    curried with apples and
        sultanas 75
    roast 62
    sausages 64
pizza
    dough 155
    frozen 19
Plain Shelf 11, 18, 19

plums, roasted with flapjack
    topping 129
poaching 19, 96
polenta 124
pomegranate glaze for roast
    turkey 163
popovers with fruit compote 24, 25
poppadums 16
pork
    balsamic pork roast 86
    chops with honey and mustard
        58
    crackling roast pork 84
    oven-roasted spare ribs 86, 87
    roasting 80
porridge 23
potatoes
    Aga oven chips 56
    Alsatian potato torte 46
    baked jacket 19, 112
    dauphinoise 116
    lemon and thyme potato
        gratin 121
    mashed 112
    new, with pancetta and
        pinenuts 113
    roast 16, 17, 110-11
poussins, spatchcock 64
prawns
    grilled, and fennel salad 42-3
    prawn and pumpkin curry 101
preserving 180
prunes, prune and apple
    chutney 181
pumpkin, baked 118-19

quail, roast 62

rabbit with garlic and lemon
    zest 72-3
red cabbage, braised 121
red onion confit 184
reheating food 16
rice
    cheese and rice soufflé 173
    coconut rice pudding 137
    cooking 12, 19, 124

acknowledgements

A huge thank you to Denise Bates and the Ebury team, everyone at Aga-Rayburn and Agalinks,
Kevin Mangeolles, Jacki Everset, Laurence Coates, John and Steph Illsley, Maureen Mills, Sarah Wooldridge,
Catherine Holloway, and last, but not least, my family, Jeremy, Harriet and Charlotte.